# Endangered Oceans

# Other Books of Related Interest:

## Opposing Viewpoints Series

Corporate Social Responsibility

The Environment

Natural Disasters

## At Issue Series

Are Natural Disasters Increasing?

Can Glacier and Ice Melt Be Reversed?

Fracking

## Current Controversies Series

Global Warming

Oil Spills

Pesticides

"Congress shall make no law . . . abridging the freedom of speech, or of the press."

*First Amendment to the US Constitution*

The basic foundation of our democracy is the First Amendment guarantee of freedom of expression. The Opposing Viewpoints Series is dedicated to the concept of this basic freedom and the idea that it is more important to practice it than to enshrine it.

# Endangered Oceans

*Helga Schier and Lynn M. Zott, Book Editors*

**GREENHAVEN PRESS**
*A part of Gale, Cengage Learning*

Farmington Hills, Mich • San Francisco • New York • Waterville, Maine
Meriden, Conn • Mason, Ohio • Chicago

Elizabeth Des Chenes, *Director, Content Strategy*
Cynthia Sanner, *Publisher*
Douglas Dentino, *Manager, New Product*

*For more information, contact:*
Greenhaven Press
27500 Drake Rd.
Farmington Hills, MI 48331-3535
Or you can visit our Internet site at gale.cengage.com

For product information and technology assistance, contact us at

Gale Customer Support, 1-800-877-4253
For permission to use material from this text or product, submit all requests online at www.cengage.com/permissions

Further permissions questions can be emailed to permissionrequest@cengage.com

Articles in Greenhaven Press anthologies are often edited for length to meet page requirements. In addition, original titles of these works are changed to clearly present the main thesis and to explicitly indicate the author's opinion. Every effort is made to ensure that Greenhaven Press accurately reflects the original intent of the authors. Every effort has been made to trace the owners of copyrighted material.

Cover image copyright © Stephen Frink Collection/Alamy.

**LIBRARY OF CONGRESS CATALOGING-IN-PUBLICATION DATA**

Endangered oceans / Helga Schier and Lynn M. Zott, book editors.
    pages cm. -- (Opposing viewpoints)
    Includes bibliographical references and index.
    ISBN 978-0-7377-6052-1 (hardcover) -- ISBN 978-0-7377-6053-8 (pbk.)
  1. Marine ecology. 2. Endangered ecosystems. 3. Marine resources conservation.
4. Sustainable fisheries. I. Schier, Helga, editor of compilation. II. Zott, Lynn M.
(Lynn Marie), 1969- editor of compilation.
  QH541.5.S3E535 2014
  577.7--dc23
                                    2013036418

# Contents

## Chapter 3: What Strategies Would Best Promote Sustainable Fishing?

## Chapter 4: What Impact Do Human Activities Have on Marine Mammals?

# Why Consider
# Opposing Viewpoints?

> *"The only way in which a human being can make some approach to knowing the whole of a subject is by hearing what can be said about it by persons of every variety of opinion and studying all modes in which it can be looked at by every character of mind. No wise man ever acquired his wisdom in any mode but this."*
>
> *John Stuart Mill*

In our media-intensive culture it is not difficult to find differing opinions. Thousands of newspapers and magazines and dozens of radio and television talk shows resound with differing points of view. The difficulty lies in deciding which opinion to agree with and which "experts" seem the most credible. The more inundated we become with differing opinions and claims, the more essential it is to hone critical reading and thinking skills to evaluate these ideas. Opposing Viewpoints books address this problem directly by presenting stimulating debates that can be used to enhance and teach these skills. The varied opinions contained in each book examine many different aspects of a single issue. While examining these conveniently edited opposing views, readers can develop critical thinking skills such as the ability to compare and contrast authors' credibility, facts, argumentation styles, use of persuasive techniques, and other stylistic tools. In short, the Opposing Viewpoints Series is an ideal way to attain the higher-level thinking and reading skills so essential in a culture of diverse and contradictory opinions.

In addition to providing a tool for critical thinking, Opposing Viewpoints books challenge readers to question their own strongly held opinions and assumptions. Most people form their opinions on the basis of upbringing, peer pressure, and personal, cultural, or professional bias. By reading carefully balanced opposing views, readers must directly confront new ideas as well as the opinions of those with whom they disagree. This is not to argue simplistically that everyone who reads opposing views will—or should—change his or her opinion. Instead, the series enhances readers' understanding of their own views by encouraging confrontation with opposing ideas. Careful examination of others' views can lead to the readers' understanding of the logical inconsistencies in their own opinions, perspective on why they hold an opinion, and the consideration of the possibility that their opinion requires further evaluation.

## Evaluating Other Opinions

To ensure that this type of examination occurs, Opposing Viewpoints books present all types of opinions. Prominent spokespeople on different sides of each issue as well as well-known professionals from many disciplines challenge the reader. An additional goal of the series is to provide a forum for other, less known, or even unpopular viewpoints. The opinion of an ordinary person who has had to make the decision to cut off life support from a terminally ill relative, for example, may be just as valuable and provide just as much insight as a medical ethicist's professional opinion. The editors have two additional purposes in including these less known views. One, the editors encourage readers to respect others' opinions—even when not enhanced by professional credibility. It is only by reading or listening to and objectively evaluating others' ideas that one can determine whether they are worthy of consideration. Two, the inclusion of such viewpoints encourages the important critical thinking skill of objectively evaluating an author's credentials and bias. This evaluation will illuminate an author's reasons for taking a particular stance on an issue and will aid in readers' evaluation of the author's ideas.

It is our hope that these books will give readers a deeper understanding of the issues debated and an appreciation of the complexity of even seemingly simple issues when good and honest people disagree. This awareness is particularly important in a democratic society such as ours in which people enter into public debate to determine the common good. Those with whom one disagrees should not be regarded as enemies but rather as people whose views deserve careful examination and may shed light on one's own.

Thomas Jefferson once said that "difference of opinion leads to inquiry, and inquiry to truth." Jefferson, a broadly educated man, argued that "if a nation expects to be ignorant and free . . . it expects what never was and never will be." As individuals and as a nation, it is imperative that we consider the opinions of others and examine them with skill and discernment. The Opposing Viewpoints Series is intended to help readers achieve this goal.

*David L. Bender and Bruno Leone,*
*Founders*

# Introduction

> "The ocean has always been thought of as the epitome of unconquerable, inexhaustible vastness and variety, but this 'plenty more fish in the sea' image may be its worst enemy. The immense scale of the ocean, and its remoteness from most of our daily lives, has contributed to its chronic neglect."
>
> *Sidney Draggan,*
> *Stockholm Environment Institute, 2012*

The term *dead zone* is used to describe an area in the ocean with reduced levels of oxygen, which causes marine organisms to either die or take off for healthier waters, leaving behind an area with very few, if any, life forms. Dead zones are a natural phenomenon that can be caused by extreme environmental events, such as a hurricane or a flood, but often they are, to quote the National Oceanic and Atmospheric Administration, "created or enhanced by human activity. There are many physical, chemical, and biological factors that combine to create dead zones, but nutrient pollution is the primary cause of those zones created by humans. Excess nutrients that run off land or are piped as wastewater into rivers and coasts can stimulate an overgrowth of algae, which then sinks and decomposes in the water. The decomposition process consumes oxygen and depletes the supply available to healthy marine life."[1]

Contrary to what one might assume, it is not chemicals that kill off marine life in these dead zones, but an overabundance of nutrients, which cause an algae bloom that in turn depletes the water of oxygen. "The apparent cause of the creeping dead zones is agriculture, specifically fertilizer. While fertilizer is necessary to foster bumper agricultural crops, it also runs off the fields into the streams and rivers of a watershed. When the fertilizer reaches the ocean, it just becomes more nutrients for the phytoplankton, so they do what they do best: they grow and multiply. Which leads to more organic matter reaching the bottom, more bacterial respiration, and more anoxic [oxygen-starved] bottom water,"[2] says the National Aeronautics and Space Administration's Goddard Earth Sciences Data and Information Services Center.

Dead zones are increasing in number and size. According to United Nations reports, "There are now 405 identified dead zones worldwide, up from 49 in the 1960s."[3] Concern over the increase of dead zones goes far beyond the desire to ensure biodiversity. Dead zones have serious economic consequences. "A single low-oxygen event (known scientifically as hypoxia) off the coasts of New York State and New Jersey in 1976 covering a mere 385 square miles (1,000 square kilometers) of seabed ended up costing commercial and recreational fisheries in the region more than $500 million,"[4] reports David Biello of *Scientific American*.

Reducing and avoiding the creation of such dead zones requires that policy makers, environmentalists, economists, farmers, and fishers work together. "Just as society rewards farmers for conserving wildlife habitat, it should also reward them for preserving wetlands and other natural barriers that prevent agricultural fertilizer from leaving farms,"[5] says David Beckman of the Natural Resources Defense Council. Ecosystems are interrelated and interdependent, which essentially means that what happens on land affects the oceans, and vice versa. A study released by the Global Environment Facility revealed that indeed "one of the most efficient ways to reduce oxygen depletion was to stem the flow of nutrients from fertilizers, municipal sewage or livestock waste into coastal waters."[6]

Studying the effects of farming on the Upper Mississippi River Basin, the United States Department of Agriculture found that "conservation practice adoption has made good progress toward reducing sediment, nutrient, and pesticide losses from farm fields, but significant challenges remain."[7] Local farmers claim that they are already using as little fertilizer as possible. "Sometimes it's portrayed we're out here dumping fertilizer for fun. . . . But if you pay the bill, why, you don't use more than you need,"[8] says Ron Hardecke, a farmer in Montana, and Mike Geske, a farmer in Mississippi, claims that he uses "20 to 25 percent less fertilizer these days."[9]

Why should farmers, or anyone else, even care that there are dead zones in the ocean? *Valuing the Ocean*, a 2012 report conducted by an international, multidisciplinary team of experts delivered at the United Nations Conference for Sustainable Development 2012 Rio+20, provides a succinct answer: "The ocean is the cornerstone of our life-support system. It covers over 70 percent of our planet and generates the oxygen in every second breath we take; it has cushioned the blow of climate change by absorbing 25–30 percent of all anthropogenic [human-made] carbon emissions and 80 percent of the heat added to the global system; it regulates our weather and provides food for billions of people. The ocean is priceless."[10]

Dead zones may simply be the most obvious sign that something is amiss. *Valuing the Ocean* claims that

> ocean acidification, hypoxic "dead zones," sea-level rise, ocean warming, marine pollution, and overuse of marine resources comprise the "multiple stressors" that are acting in awful synergy to harm the ocean services that hold an essential if unrecognized place in our economic future. If we fail to take these stressors seriously and allow the global temperature to rise by four degrees Celsius, we risk a future of depleted fisheries, disrupted tourism, bleached coral reefs, terrifying floods, and tropical cyclones, all of which bear heavy financial and environmental costs.[11]

The study puts an actual price tag of almost $2 trillion on failure to counteract the factors that endanger our priceless oceans, calculating "the cost over the next 50 and 100 years respectively in terms of five categories of lost ocean value (fisheries, tourism, sea-level rise, storms, and the ocean carbon sink),"[12] says Sweden's Stockholm Environment Institute. In other words, if people do not take care of the oceans, everyone's checkbook will be affected.

The authors in *Opposing Viewpoints: Endangered Oceans* debate potential shifts in attitude, policy, and action, which are necessary and possible to counteract the multitude of interconnected threats facing the ocean. Some of these threats, such as overfishing, have been the subject of much research and discussion, while dangers such as ocean acidification are not yet fully understood and remain obscure to the general public. Four chapters address four pertinent questions that look at the dangers facing our oceans from various angles: What Threatens the World's Oceans?, What Ocean Policies Are Best?, What Strategies Would Best Promote Sustainable Fishing?, and What Impact Do Human Activities Have on Marine Mammals?

## Notes

1. National Oceanic and Atmospheric Administration, "Dead Zone Is a More Common Term for Hypoxia, Which Refers to a Reduced Level of Oxygen in the Water," November 17, 2011. http://oceanservice.noaa.gov/facts/deadzone.html.
2. Goddard Earth Sciences Data and Information Services Center, "Mississippi Dead Zone," August, 10, 2004. www.nasa.gov/vision/earth/environment/dead_zone.html.
3. David Biello, "Oceanic Dead Zones Continue to Spread," *Scientific American*, August 15, 2008. www.scientific american.com/article.cfm?id=oceanic-dead-zones-spread.
4. Biello, "Oceanic Dead Zones Continue to Spread."
5. David Beckman, "Solutions for Shrinking the Dead Zone in the Aftermath of the Great Flood in 2011," *Switchboard* (blog), May 24, 2011. http://switchboard.nrdc.org/blogs /dbeckman/solutions_for_shrinking_the_de.html.

6. Mishal Hardenberg Hamid, "Raising the Bar: 20 Years of GEF Transboundary Water Results," Global Environment Facility, October 2011. http://iwlearn.net /abt_iwlearn/events/conferences/iwc6/iwc6-docs/iwc6 -second-announcement.

7. USDA Natural Resources Conservation Service, "Assessment of the Effects of Conservation Practices on Cultivated Cropland in the Upper Mississippi River Basin," June 2010. www.nrcs.usda.gov/Internet/FSE _DOCUMENTS/stelprdb1042093.pdf.

8. Quoted in Sarah Sipley Hiles, "Dead Zone Pollutant Grows Despite Decades of Work. But Who's the Culprit?," Environmental Health News, July 9, 2012. http:// sarashipleyhiles.com/2012/07/10/dead-zone-pollutant -grows-despite-decades-of-work-but-whos-the-culprit/.

9. Quoted in Hiles, "Dead Zone Pollutant Grows Despite Decades of Work."

10. Kevin Noone, Rashid Sumaila, Robert J. Díaz, eds., *Valuing the Ocean*, Draft Executive Summary, Stockholm Environment Institute, 2012. www.sei-international.org /mediamanager/documents/Publications/SEI-Preview -ValuingTheOcean-DraftExecutiveSummary.pdf.

11. Quoted in Jenny Slattery, "Ocean Degradation $2 Trillion Price Tag," *Sierra Daily* (blog), April 9, 2012. http://sierraclub.typepad.com/sierradaily/2012/04/ocean -degradation-could-cost-us-2-trillion-dollars-a-year-by -2100-.html.

12. Stockholm Environment Institute, "Multiple Stressors Pushing Ocean Ecosystems, Livelihoods to the Brink," March 21, 2012. www.sei-international.org/-news -archive/2305.

OPPOSING
VIEWPOINTS®
SERIES

# CHAPTER 1

# What Threatens the World's Oceans?

# Chapter Preface

Controversy over fishing practices and their potentially harmful impact on the environment is by no means new:

> Certain fishermen for several years past have subtly contrived an instrument called "wondyrechaun" made in the manner of an oyster dredge, but which is considerably longer, upon which instrument is attached a net so close meshed that no fish, be it ever so small, that enters therein can escape, but must stay and be taken. And that the great and long iron of the wondyrechaun runs so heavily and hardly over the ground when fishing that it destroys the flowers of the land below water there, and also spat of oysters, mussels and other fish upon which the great fish are accustomed to be fed and nourished. By which instrument in many places, the fishermen take such quantity of small fish that they do not know what to do with them; and that they feed and fat their pigs with them, to the great damage of the commons of the realm and the destruction of the fisheries, and they pray for a remedy.

This quote is from a 1376 petition to King Edward III of England. The wondyrechaun, according to the petition, destroys habitats and results in bycatch so serious it endangers several species of fish, is an early version of the bottom trawl, a cone-shaped fishing net designed to be dragged along the ocean floor to catch deepwater fish.

Fast forward to 2012, where at Rio+20, the United Nations Conference on Sustainable Development, Sebastian Marino, environmental planner for the Republic of Palau, a Pacific island nation, repeats that same petition in rather simple words: "Bottom trawling must stop."

Arguments for such a ban are abundant. The Marine Conservation Institute warns:

Bottom trawling is unselective and severely damaging to benthic [seafloor] ecosystems. The net indiscriminately catches every life and object it encounters. Thus, many creatures end up mistakenly caught and thrown overboard dead or dying, including endangered fish and even vulnerable deep-sea corals which can live for several hundred years. This collateral damage, called bycatch, can amount to 90% of a trawl's total catch.

If indeed most of the catch of a bottom trawler is bycatch—that is, unwanted fish that cannot be sold but will not survive once returned to the sea—this fishing method appears wasteful and certainly not in line with attempts to sustain ocean biodiversity.

"The extensive use of bottom trawls and dredges for commercial fishing causes more direct and avoidable damage to the ocean floor—including deep-sea coral and sponge communities and other unique and sensitive seafloor marine life—than any other human activity in the world," argues Oceana, an international ocean preservation organization. The international environmental organization Greenpeace calls bottom trawling the "number 1 threat" to all deepwater life forms.

Nevertheless, appeals to ban bottom trawling have failed as recently as 2006, when the United Nations General Assembly did not include a prohibition of bottom trawling in its resolution for sustainable fishery practices. Instead, several countries have selectively restricted the practice. In 2006, the United States National Oceanic and Atmospheric Administration banned bottom trawling along the Pacific coastline of the United States up to three hundred miles off the coast; in 2005 the European Union closed off selected coastlines in Scotland; the UN Food and Agriculture Organization's General Fisheries Commission for the Mediterranean banned bottom trawling deeper than a kilometer. Other selective restrictions apply in Norway, Canada, New Zealand, and Australia.

Bottom trawls catch shrimp, cod, haddock, flounder, scallops, and clams, all fish that can be found on dinner plates around the world. Seafish, an organization representing the British seafood industry, contends that bottom trawling has come under unfair scrutiny: "No species have become extinct as a result of bottom trawling," it points out, arguing that "the designs of trawls can vary widely" and thus could be adjusted to avoid bycatch and cause less damage to ocean habitats. Seafish calls bottom trawling "a very efficient method of catching fish." The Spanish General Fisheries Confederation also opposes a unilateral condemnation of bottom trawling. "There is no good or bad gear. All the fishing methods have some impact on the environment, like any economic activity. What makes it good or bad is the use made of the gear and the regulation that is set," it argues.

Bottom trawling is but one example of human activity that threatens the world's oceans. The viewpoints in the following chapter debate other threats to the oceans, such as acidification, overfishing, pollution, and oil drilling.

> "*Eventually, all that will be left in the oceans are organisms that people won't, or can't, consume, like sea slugs and toxic algae.*"

# Overfishing Is Hazardous to Oceans

*Elizabeth Kolbert*

*Elizabeth Kolbert is a journalist and environmental commentator. In the following viewpoint she uses the example of the bluefin tuna to show that overfishing is dangerous to entire species of fish. Consumer demand creates the need for extensive fishing, which, if mismanaged, leads to a species' annihilation Kolbert declares. For centuries people developed ever more successful fishing technologies, she explains, which have disturbed the delicate balance between predator and prey. Even human-made construction not related to fishing—such as dams and mills—wreaks havoc on the natural habitats of fish, according to Kolbert, who contends that the ocean can be saved only by creating marine protected areas.*

As you read, consider the following questions:

1. According to the author, how much did a five-hundred-pound bluefin sell for in 2010 at a Tokyo auction?

2. According to Kolbert, where was the Great International Fisheries Exhibition in 1883?

3. In the author's opinion, how far did British fishing boats sail for fishing in the fifteenth century?

The Atlantic bluefin tuna is shaped like a child's idea of a fish, with a pointy snout, two dorsal fins, and a rounded belly that gradually tapers toward the back. It is gunmetal blue on top, and silvery on the underside, and its tail looks like a sickle. The Atlantic bluefin is one of the fastest swimmers in the sea, reaching speeds of fifty-five miles an hour. This is an achievement that scientists have sought to understand but have never quite mastered; a robo-tuna, built by a team of engineers at M.I.T. [Massachusetts Institute of Technology], was unable to outswim a real one. (The word "tuna" is derived from the Greek *thuno*, meaning "to rush.") Atlantic bluefins are voracious carnivores—they feed on squid, crustaceans, and other fish—and can grow to be fifteen feet long.

## From Plentiful to Rare

At one time, Atlantic bluefins were common from the coast of Maine to the Black Sea, and from Norway to Brazil. In the Mediterranean, they have been prized for millennia—in an ode from the second century, the poet Oppian describes the Romans catching bluefins in "nets arranged like a city"—but they are unusually bloody fish, and in most of the rest of the world there was little market for them. (Among English speakers, they were long known as "horse mackerel.") As recently as the late nineteen-sixties, bluefin in the United States sold for only a few pennies a pound, if there were any buyers, and frequently ended up being ground into cat food. Then, in the nineteen-seventies, the Japanese developed a taste for sushi made with bluefin, or *hon-maguro*. This new preference, it's been hypothesized, arose from their exposure, following the Second World War, to American-style fatty foods. The taste for *hon-maguro* was, in turn, imported back to the U.S. Soon, fishing for bluefin became so lucrative that the sale of a single animal could feed a family for a year. (Earlier this year [2010], a five-hundred-pound Pacific bluefin went for an astonishing three hundred and forty dollars a pound [$170,000] at a Tokyo fish auction.) First, the big bluefins were fished out, then the smaller ones, too, became hard to find. Tuna "ranching," a practice by which the fish are herded into huge circular nets and fattened up before slaughter, was for a time seen as a solution until it was shown to be part of the problem: as fewer bluefins were allowed to reach spawning age, there were fewer and fewer new fish to fatten.

Bluefin catches are managed—the word is used here loosely—by the International Commission for the Conservation of Atlantic Tunas. The commission, known by the acronym ICCAT—pronounced "eye-cat"—is based in Madrid, and its members include the U.S., the European Union, Japan, Canada, and Brazil. In 2008, ICCAT scientists recommended that the bluefin catch in the eastern Atlantic and the Mediterranean be limited to between eighty-five hundred and fifteen thousand tons. ICCAT instead adopted a quota of twenty-two thousand tons. That same year, a panel of independent reviewers, hired by the commission to assess its performance, observed that ICCAT "is widely regarded as an international disgrace." (Carl Safina, the noted marine conservationist, has nicknamed the group the International Conspiracy to Catch All the Tunas.) By most estimates, bluefin stocks have fallen by eighty per cent in the past forty years [since the 1970s]. According to other assessments, the situation is even grimmer. Callum Roberts, a professor of marine conservation at England's University of York, has calculated that there is now only one bluefin left for every fifty that were swimming in the Atlantic in 1940.

Last year [in 2009], in an effort to save the Atlantic bluefin from annihilation, Monaco proposed that the fish join animals like the giant panda and the Asian elephant on a list of creatures that cannot be traded—either alive or cut up for parts—across international borders. When the proposal came up for a vote at a U.N. meeting in Doha [Qatar] this past March, the U.S. voted in favor of it. "The science is compelling," Tom Strickland, the Assistant Secretary of the Interior for Fish, Wildlife, and Parks, told the *[New York] Times*. "That species is in spectacular decline." Nevertheless, the measure was defeated. (The vote—sixty-eight to twenty, with thirty nations abstaining—was widely seen as a victory for Japan.) The following month, the Deepwater Horizon rig exploded, and oil began gushing into the Gulf of Mexico. The Gulf is one of only two known Atlantic bluefin spawning sites, and April is the start of the spawning season.

## Fished into Oblivion

If the Atlantic bluefin tuna were the first species to be fished into oblivion, its destruction would be shameful. But, of course, its story has become routine. Cod, once so plentiful off the coast of Newfoundland that they could be scooped up in baskets, are now scarce. The same goes for halibut, haddock, swordfish, marlin, and skate; it's been calculated that stocks of large predatory fish have declined by ninety per cent in the past half century. In 1943, Rachel Carson was a young biologist working for the U.S. Fish and Wildlife Service when she wrote a booklet titled "Food from the Sea." The point of the boosterish guide was to convince American consumers of the delectableness of fish like the wolffish, an enormous creature with a bulbous head, big teeth, and an eel-like body. Wolffish is "one of New England's underexploited fishes, a condition that will be corrected when housewives discover its excellence," Carson wrote. Apparently, she was so persuasive— and bottom trawling so wrecked its habitat—that the wolffish is now considered a threatened species.

The sorry state of ocean life has led to a new kind of fish story—a lament not for the one that got away but for the countless others that didn't. In "Saved by the Sea: A Love Story with Fish," David Helvarg notes that each year sharks kill some five to eight humans worldwide; meanwhile we kill a hundred million of them. Dean Bavington, the author of "Managed Annihilation: An Unnatural History of the New-foundland Cod Collapse," observes that two hundred billion pounds' worth of cod were taken from Canada's Grand Banks before 1992, when the cod simply ran out. In "Four Fish: The Future of the Last Wild Food," Paul Greenberg estimates that somewhere in the range of a hundred million salmon larvae used to hatch in the Connecticut River each year. Now the number's a lot easier to pin down: it's zero. "The broad, complex genetic potential of the Connecticut River salmon," Greenberg writes, has "vanished from the face of the earth."

## The "Inexhaustible Sea" Is a Myth

The Great International Fisheries Exhibition, which took place in London in 1883, was a celebration of all things piscatorial [fish-related]. More than two thousand exhibitors from around the world displayed herring nets and salmon ladders, trout rods and eel spears, life buoys and lamprey baskets. Awards—dozens of them were bestowed—included twenty pounds sterling for the best collection of smoked fish, twenty-five pounds for the best model of a sailing trawler, and ten pounds for the "best Apparatus for, or Method of, protecting Young Brood and Oysters against Dog Whelks and other natural enemies."

[English biologist] Thomas Huxley, who is now mostly remembered for being an early supporter of [English naturalist] Charles Darwin, was at the time the president of Britain's Royal Society [the UK's professional science society], and he delivered the exhibition's opening address. As his topic, Huxley chose the question "Are fisheries exhaustible? That is to say, can all the fish which naturally inhabit a given area be extirpated by the agency of man?" The answer, Huxley decided, was a qualified no. Although people might be able to wipe out the salmon in a certain stream by throwing a net across it "in such a manner as to catch every salmon that tries to go up and every smolt [newly hatched salmon] that tries to go down," conditions in the ocean were altogether different.

"Probably all the great sea fisheries are inexhaustible; that is to say that nothing we do seriously affects the number of the fish," Huxley declared. To the extent that there was a problem with the fishing industry, it was due to its "relative backwardness." Fishing, Huxley said, had failed "to keep pace with the rapid improvement of almost every other branch of industrial occupation in modern times" and still lagged "very far behind scientific agriculture . . . as to the application of machinery."

Huxley's views dominated thinking about fisheries for most of the next century. In 1955, Francis Minot, the director of the Marine and Fisheries Engineering Research Institute, in Woods Hole, Massachusetts, co-wrote a book titled "The Inexhaustible Sea." As yet, he observed, "we do not know the ocean well enough. Much must still be learned. Nevertheless, we are already beginning to understand that what it has to offer extends beyond the limits of our imagination." In 1964, the annual global catch totalled around fifty million tons; a U.S. Interior Department report from that year predicted that it could be "increased at least tenfold without endangering aquatic stocks." Three years later, the department revised its estimate; the catch could be increased not by a factor of ten but by a factor of forty, to two billion tons a year. This, it noted, would be enough to feed the world's population ten times over. Michael L. Weber observes, in "From Abundance to Scarcity" (2002), that as recently as the nineteen-nineties U.S. policy was predicated "on the belief that the ocean's productivity was almost limitless."

## Technology Creates a Mismatch

In the meantime, "machinery" beyond Huxley's wildest imagining was being developed. Purse seines [circular fishing nets that are gathered together at the top by drawstrings, like a purse] were introduced in the nineteen-thirties. These giant nets can be played out around entire schools of fish, then gathered up with drawstrings, like huge laundry bags. Factory freezer trawlers [fishing vessels with onboard freezing facilities], developed after the Second World War, grew to be so gargantuan that they amounted to, in effect, seafaring towns. In the nineteen-fifties, many fleets added echo-sounding sonar, which can detect fish schools long before they surface. Today, specially designed buoys known as "fish aggregating devices," or FADs, are deployed to attract species like yellowfin tuna and blue marlin. So-called "smart" FADs come equipped with sonar and G.P.S., so operators can detect from afar whether they are, in fact, surrounded by fish.

In the short term, the new technology worked, much as Huxley had predicted, to swell catches. But only in the short term. In the late nineteen-eighties, the total world catch topped out at around eighty-five million tons, which is to say, roughly 1.9 billion tons short of the Interior Department's most lunatic estimate. This milestone—the point of what might be called "peak fish"—was passed without anyone's quite realizing it, owing to inflated catch figures from the Chinese. (These fishy figures were later exposed as politically motivated fabrications.) For the past two decades, the global catch has been steadily declining. It is estimated that the total take is dropping by around five hundred thousand tons a year.

Meanwhile, as the size of the catch has fallen, so, too, has the size of the creatures being caught. This phenomenon, which has become known as "fishing down the food web," was first identified by Daniel Pauly, a fisheries biologist at the University of British Columbia. In "Five Easy Pieces: How Fishing Impacts Marine Ecosystems," Pauly follows this trend to its

## Fishing Thwarts Fish Evolution

Overfishing may . . . interfere with evolution. By targeting big fish for harvest and throwing back or ignoring small ones, some scientists believe humans are artificially selecting for fish with small bodies—since diminutive fish are more likely to survive and therefore reproduce more often, they also pass on more genes than their bigger, meatier relatives. Markets reportedly sold cod 100 years ago that measured nearly five feet long, but the largest cod today are around 20 inches.

*Russell McLendan, Mother Nature Network,*
*October 6, 2009. www.mnn.com.*

logical—or, if you prefer, illogical—conclusion. Eventually, all that will be left in the oceans are organisms that people won't, or can't, consume, like sea slugs and toxic algae. It's been argued that humans have become such a dominant force on the planet that we've ushered in a new geological epoch. Pauly proposes that this new epoch be called the Myxocene, from the Greek *muxa*, meaning "slime."

The new fish stories can be read as parables about technology. What was, once upon a time, a stable relationship between predator and prey was transformed by new "machinery" into a deadly mismatch. This reading isn't so much wrong as misleading. To paraphrase the old N.R.A. [National Rifle Association] favorite, FADs don't kill fish, people do.

## Humans Have Ever Exploited the Sea

In an effort to figure out what ocean life was like before the modern era, marine scientists have, in the past few decades, cored through seafloor sediments, measured the size of fish bones tossed out at ancient banquets, and combed through the logs of early explorers. As Callum Roberts reports in "The Unnatural History of the Sea" (2007), the work suggests that humans have been wreaking havoc in the oceans for centuries.

Consider the example of Britain. Archeological deposits show that around the year 1000 Europe's freshwater fisheries were already in decline, perhaps owing to overfishing or perhaps to the erection of dams and mills that impeded river flows. To make a living, British fishermen set out to sea. Initially, the marine catch appears to have been bountiful; analysis of what might be described as eleventh-century garbage shows that people in what is now Scotland dined on four-foot-long cod and five-foot-long pollack. But gradually local stocks were fished down, and by the fifteenth century British ships were venturing as far away as Norway and Iceland. (The Danes, who claimed Iceland for themselves, complained that the English were setting up entire villages on the island, "putting up tents, digging ditches, working away.") When, in the early sixteenth century, British fishermen turned their attention to the newly discovered fisheries off Newfoundland, they encountered, in the words of one early settler, "Cods so thicke by the shoare that we heardlie have been able to row a Boate through them," and the cycle began all over again.

At this point, there are probably no new fishing grounds to be discovered, or, to use Rachel Carson's phrase, any "underexploited fishes" to start serving for dinner. (In parts of Asia, jellyfish are already considered a delicacy.) After the collapse of so many freshwater fish, migratory fish, oceanic fish, and groundfish, like the wolffish, it might seem that we've finally reached the end of the line.

## Marine Protected Areas Can Save the Sea

And yet this is never where the new fish stories, or stories about the fish stories, wind up. Just when things seem bleakest, hope—dolphinlike—swims into the picture. David Helvarg concludes his memoir-cum-ecological-disaster narrative

"Saved by the Sea" by declaring that, owing to a new attitude in Washington, things seem "to be looking up for the ocean." Similarly, Roberts closes his chronicle of more than a millennium of overfishing by asserting, "We can restore the life and habits of the sea because it is in everyone's interest that we do so."

The way to keep fishing, according to Roberts, lies in not fishing—or, at least, in not fishing everywhere. He proposes that huge swaths of the sea be set aside as so-called "marine protected areas," or M.P.A.s, where most commercial activity would be prohibited. In "Four Fish," Paul Greenberg argues that the salvation of wild fish lies in farmed ones, though not in the kind you'll find on ice at Stop & Shop. (Today, most farmed fish are fed on wild-caught fish, a practice that only exacerbates the problem.) Greenberg is a believer in what's sometimes called "smart aquaculture," and thinks we should be eating species like *Pangasius hypophthalmus*, commonly known as tra. Tra happily feed on human waste and were originally kept in Southeast Asia to dispose of the contents of outhouses. Michael Weber, the author of "From Abundance to Scarcity," is encouraged by the introduction of new regulatory mechanisms such as "individual transferable quotas," or I.T.Q.s. The idea behind I.T.Q.s is that if fishermen are granted a marketable stake in the catch they will have a greater economic interest in preserving it.

M.P.A.s, smart aquaculture, and I.T.Q.s—these are all worthy proposals that, if instituted on a large enough scale, would probably make a difference. As Roberts notes, it is in "everyone's interest" to take the steps needed to prevent an ocean-wide slide into slime. But it is also in everyone's interest to save the Atlantic bluefin tuna. Still, it is being fished to the edge of extinction, which is why a hopeful ending is not always the most convincing one.

| *"For the first time in at least a century, U.S. fishermen are not taking too much of any species from the sea."*

# Overfishing Is No Longer a Danger to Oceans

### Gloucester Times

*In the following viewpoint from the* Gloucester Times *of Gloucester, Massachusetts, the staff writer discusses the work of Steve Murawski, a fisheries biologist and marine ecologist at the University of South Florida. Murawski claims that the new catch share program (in which fishing boats share catches with other boats) has ended overfishing in New England. He argues that enforcing the Magnuson-Stevens Act in New England, which imposes strict catch limits and encourages a catch share program, has increased the fish stock in 2010. Despite its potential dangers to smaller fishing boats, Murawski asserts, the results of the catch share program show that management programs can end overfishing. Once fishing boats continuously fish at a sustainable rate, he concludes, regulations can and should be loosened again.*

As you read, consider the following questions:

1. According to the author, when did people start keeping written records of fishing history?

2. When does the *Times* writer claim fishermen will be forced to stop fishing altogether, under the New England catch share program?

3. In the author's opinion, what variable can sometimes boost the stock of a specific species?

For the first time in at least a century, U.S. fishermen are not taking too much of any species from the sea, one of the nation's top fishery scientists says.

The projected end of overfishing comes during a turbulent fishing year [2010] that's seen fishermen out of Gloucester and throughout New England switch to the radically new catch share management system.

But scientist Steve Murawski said that, for the first time in written fishing history, which goes back to 1900, "As far as we know, we've hit the right levels, which is a milestone."

"And this isn't just a decadal [ten-year] milestone, this is a century phenomenon," said Murawski, who retired last week as chief scientist at the National Oceanic and Atmospheric Administration's Fisheries Service.

Murawski said it's more than a dramatic benchmark—it also signals increasingly healthy stocks and perhaps better days for fishermen who've suffered financially. In New England, the fleet has deteriorated since the mid-1990s from 1,200 boats to only about 580, but Murawski believes fishermen may have already endured their worst times.

"I honestly think that's true, and that's why I think it's a newsworthy event," said Murawski, now a professor at the University of South Florida.

Fishermen and their advocates, however, say the documented end to "overfishing" has come at an unnecessarily high cost.

Dave Marciano, who fished out of Gloucester for three decades until he was forced to sell his commercial fishing permit last June [2010], said the new catch share system has simply made it too costly to catch enough fish to stay in business.

"It ruined me," Marciano, 45, said of the catch share management scheme. "We could have ended overfishing and had a lot more consideration for the human side of the fishery."

An end to overfishing doesn't mean all stocks are healthy, but scientists believe it's a crucial step to getting there.

## The Magnuson-Stevens Act

When fishermen are overfishing a species, they're catching it at a rate scientists believe is too fast to ensure that the species can rebuild and then stay healthy. It's different from when a species is overfished, which is when scientists believe its population is too low.

Murawski said it's a nearly ironclad rule of fishery management that species become far more abundant when they're being fished at the appropriate level, which is determined after considering factors such as a species' life span and death rates.

A mandate to end overfishing by the 2010 fishing year—which, in the New England groundfishery, began last May 1 [2010] and runs through April 30 [2011]—came in the 2006 reauthorization of the nation's fisheries law, the Magnuson-Stevens Act.

Murawski said the U.S. is the only country that has a law that defines overfishing and requires its fishermen not to engage in it.

"When you compare the United States with the European Union, with Asian countries, et cetera, we are the only industrialized fishing nation who actually has succeeded in ending overfishing," he said.

## New England's Catch Share Program

Regulators say 37 stocks nationwide last year were being overfished (counting only those that live exclusively in U.S. waters); New England had the most with 10. But Murawski said management systems that emphasize strict catch limits have made a big difference, and New England just made the switch.

Under the new catch share program, New England's fishermen work in cooperative groups called sectors to divide an annual quota of the groundfish stocks, including cod, haddock and flounder.

If they exceed their limits on one species, they're forced to stop fishing on all species. Fishermen under the catch share system are encouraged to buy, sell or trade their "shares" of the total allowable catch among themselves or to outside investment interests, much like a commodities market. That has been consolidating control of the fishing resources in the hands of the bigger boats and corporations, and at the expense of the smaller, independent fishermen and boat owners, critics say.

About two-thirds into the current fishing year, which ends April 30, federal data indicated New England fishermen were on pace to catch fewer than their allotted fish in all but one stock, Georges Bank winter flounder. But Murawski said he didn't expect fishermen would exceed their quota on any stock.

In other regions with documented overfishing—the South Atlantic, the Gulf of Mexico and the Caribbean—regulators project catch limits and other measures will end overfishing this fishing year as well. Already, South Atlantic black grouper and Gulf of Mexico red snapper are no longer being overfished.

The final verification that overfishing has ended nationwide, at least for one fishing year, will come after detailed stock assessments.

## A Pyrrhic Victory

That will be a "Pyrrhic victory" [a victory that came at a high cost to the victor] in hard-hit New England, said Brian Rothschild, the dean of marine science at the University of Massachusetts at Dartmouth, and a respected figure throughout the industry.

## Regulation, Not Overfishing, Is the Problem

Overfishing simply isn't happening. Our already pathetically small fishing industry is rapidly declining as the burden of regulation drives fishermen to give up and deters newcomers from starting. Apart from a few of the most lucrative export fisheries, the quotas and licences fishermen were led to believe would be their retirement fund have been rendered worthless by restrictions and demands. Worse yet, they have become costly liabilities to maintain. In the most valuable fisheries licences and quotas are increasingly being bought up by investors and the resource owned by absentee landlords. While their share croppers do the fishing, these new landed gentry groom the bureaucratic overlords for indulgences. The 21st century is the new Middle Ages.

*Walter Starck,* Walter Starck's Blog, *June 2009.*
*www.bairdmaritime.com.*

He said regulators could legally loosen the rules and allow fishermen to safely catch more fish, but regulators have refused to do so, and Secretary of Commerce Gary Locke reiterated that stand [in January 2011], formally rejecting a request from [Massachusetts] Gov. Deval Patrick to grant additional allocations owing to an economic emergency for the fishing industry and fishing communities like Gloucester and New Bedford.

Because of that, Rothschild says, fishermen have needlessly been shut out from even healthy stocks.

Marciano notes that the fishery science is far from perfect.

Regulators believed fishermen were overfishing pollock until new data last year indicated scientists had badly underestimated its population, he noted, leading federal regulators to already boost that limit by 600 percent.

And some stocks, such as Gulf of Maine cod, have recovered even when fishermen were technically overfishing them.

"To say you can't rebuild stocks while overfishing is occurring is an outright lie," Marciano said. "We did it."

Tom Nies, a fisheries analyst for regional New England regulators, said stocks can sometimes be boosted by variables such as strong births in a given year, but they'll inevitably decline if overfishing continues on them.

And Peter Shelley, senior counsel of the Conservation Law Foundation, said the industry's problems are rooted in years of overfishing, especially during the 1980s, not regulation.

"It was a bubble," he said. "Fishermen were living in a bit of a fantasy world at that point, and it wasn't something you could sustain."

That's why Murawski's projection about the end of overfishing is "a very big deal," he said.

## An Uncertain Future Lies Ahead

"I think we're just starting to see signs of a new future," Shelley said.

Yet fisherman Steve Arnold, 46, says all he sees in his home port of Point Judith, R.I., are fewer boats, older fishermen and "a lot of frowns on people's faces."

Overfishing might end this year, but the fleet has suffered and has an uncertain future, he said.

"I believe we can get to a better place, but the work isn't done," Arnold said. "We're living through something that we're learning as we go. It's not a comfortable feeling."

*"The carbon dioxide we have put into the atmosphere since the Industrial Revolution has lowered the ocean pH level."*

# Carbon Emissions Cause Dangerous Ocean Acidification

*Carl Zimmer*

*Carl Zimmer is a science lecturer at Yale University. In the following viewpoint, he argues that the burning of fossil fuels ultimately causes the extinction of marine species. The absence of certain fossilized shelled creatures in ocean sediments dating 55 million years ago, he explains, is because of past acidification's causing the extinction of the species. Carbon dioxide in the air increases the acidity of seawater, which hinders shell-building in some single-cell organisms, Zimmer asserts. Extinction of these species disturbs the food chain and destabilizes the ecosystem, according to Zimmer, who concludes from experiments that there are similarities between the past and current carbon dioxide jolt and the acidification levels of oceans, which warns of extinction of species to come.*

As you read, consider the following questions:

1. According to the author, what does the discovery of red clay within a white sediment on the ocean floor signify?

2. What is the typical pH level on the ocean's surface, according to the author?

3. According to Zimmer, what factors show that the ancient catastrophe he describes is not a perfect prequel to today's circumstances?

The *JOIDES Resolution* looks like a bizarre hybrid of an oil rig and a cargo ship. It is, in fact, a research vessel that ocean scientists use to dig up sediment from the sea floor. In 2003, on a voyage to the southeastern Atlantic, scientists aboard the *JOIDES Resolution* brought up a particularly striking haul.

They had drilled down into sediment that had formed on the sea floor over the course of millions of years. The oldest sediment in the drill was white. It had been formed by the calcium carbonate shells of single-celled organisms—the same kind of material that makes up the White Cliffs of Dover [in England]. But when the scientists examined the sediment that had formed 55 million years ago, the color changed in a geological blink of an eye.

"In the middle of this white sediment, there's this big plug of red clay," says Andy Ridgwell, an earth scientist at the University of Bristol.

In other words, the vast clouds of shelled creatures in the deep oceans had virtually disappeared. Many scientists now agree that this change was caused by a drastic drop of the ocean's pH level [a measure of acidity]. The seawater became so corrosive that it ate away at the shells, along with other species with calcium carbonate in their bodies. It took hundreds of thousands of years for the oceans to recover from this crisis, and for the sea floor to turn from red back to white.

## Current Ocean Acidity Levels

The clay that the crew of the *JOIDES Resolution* dredged up may be an ominous warning of what the future has in store. By spewing carbon dioxide into the air, we are now once again making the oceans more acidic.

Today, Ridgwell and Daniela Schmidt, also of the University of Bristol, are publishing a study in the journal *Natural Geoscience*, comparing what happened in the oceans 55 million years ago to what the oceans are experiencing today. Their research supports what other researchers have long suspected: The acidification of the ocean today is bigger and faster than anything geologists can find in the fossil record over the past 65 million years. Indeed, its speed and strength—Ridgwell estimates that current ocean acidification is taking place at ten times the rate that preceded the mass extinction 55 million years ago—may spell doom for many marine species, particularly ones that live in the deep ocean.

"This is an almost unprecedented geological event," says Ridgwell.

## Carbon Dioxide Acidifies Seawater

When we humans burn fossil fuels, we pump carbon dioxide into the atmosphere, where the gas traps heat. But much of that carbon dioxide does not stay in the air. Instead, it gets sucked into the oceans. If not for the oceans, climate scientists believe that the planet would be much warmer than it is today. Even with the oceans' massive uptake of $CO_2$, the past decade was still the warmest since modern record-keeping began. But storing carbon dioxide in the oceans may come at a steep cost: It changes the chemistry of seawater.

At the ocean's surface, seawater typically has a pH of about 8 to 8.3 pH units. For comparison, the pH of pure water is 7, and stomach acid is around 2. The pH level of a liquid is determined by how many positively charged hydrogen atoms are floating around in it. The more hydrogen ions, the lower the pH. When carbon dioxide enters the ocean, it lowers the pH by reacting with water.

The carbon dioxide we have put into the atmosphere since the Industrial Revolution has lowered the ocean pH level by .1. That may seem tiny, but it's not. The pH scale is logarithmic, meaning that there are 10 times more hydrogen ions in a pH 5 liquid than one at pH 6, and 100 times more than pH 7. As a result, a drop of just .1 pH units means that the concentration of hydrogen ions in the ocean has gone up by about 30 percent in the past two centuries.

## Acidification Upsets Ocean Ecosystems

To see how ocean acidification is going to affect life in the ocean, scientists have run laboratory experiments in which they rear organisms at different pH levels. The results have been worrying—particularly for species that build skeletons out of calcium carbonate, such as corals and amoeba-like organisms called foraminifera. The extra hydrogen in low-pH seawater reacts with calcium carbonate, turning it into other compounds that animals can't use to build their shells.

These results are worrisome, not just for the particular species the scientists study, but for the ecosystems in which they live. Some of these vulnerable species are crucial for entire ecosystems in the ocean. Small shell-building organisms are food for invertebrates [animals without a spine], such as mollusks, and small fish, which in turn are food for larger predators. Coral reefs create an underwater rain forest, cradling a quarter of the ocean's biodiversity.

But on their own, lab experiments lasting for a few days or weeks may not tell scientists how ocean acidification will affect the entire planet. "It's not obvious what these mean in the real world," says Ridgwell.

## Flooding the Oceans with $CO_2$

One way to get more information is to look at the history of the oceans themselves, which is what Ridgwell and Schmidt have done in their new study. At first glance, that history might suggest we have nothing to worry about. A hundred million years ago, there was over five times more carbon dioxide in the atmosphere and the ocean was .8 pH units lower. Yet there was plenty of calcium carbonate for foraminifera and other species. It was during this period, in fact, that shell-building marine organisms produced the limestone formations that would eventually become the White Cliffs of Dover.

But there's a crucial difference between the Earth 100 million years ago and today. Back then, carbon dioxide concentrations changed very slowly over millions of years. Those slow changes triggered other slow changes in the Earth's chemistry. For example, as the planet warmed from more carbon dioxide, the increased rainfall carried more minerals from the mountains into the ocean, where they could alter the chemistry of the seawater. Even at low pH, the ocean contains enough dissolved calcium carbonate for corals and other species to survive.

Today, however, we are flooding the atmosphere with carbon dioxide at a rate rarely seen in the history of our planet. The planet's weathering feedbacks won't be able to compensate for the sudden drop in pH for hundreds of thousands of years.

## Clues in the Fossil Record

Scientists have been scouring the fossil record for periods of history that might offer clues to how the planet will respond to the current carbon jolt. They've found that 55 million years ago, the Earth went through a similar change. Lee Kump of Penn State [University] and his colleagues have estimated that roughly 6.8 trillion tons of carbon entered the Earth's atmosphere over about 10,000 years.

Nobody can say for sure what unleashed all that carbon, but it appeared to have had a drastic effect on the climate. Temperatures rose between 5 and 9 degrees Celsius (9 to 16 Fahrenheit). Many deep-water species became extinct, possibly as the pH of the deep ocean became too low for them to survive.

But this ancient catastrophe (known as the Paleocene-Eocene thermal maximum, or PETM) was not a perfect prequel to what's happening on Earth today. The temperature was warmer before the carbon bomb went off, and the pH of the oceans was lower. The arrangement of the continents was also different. The winds blew in different patterns as a result, driving the oceans in different directions. All these factors make a big difference on the effect of ocean acidification. For example, the effect that low pH has on skeleton-building organisms depends on the pressure and temperature of the ocean. Below a certain depth in the ocean, the water becomes so cold and the pressure so high that there's no calcium carbonate left for shell-building organisms. That threshold is known as the saturation horizon.

## Comparing the PETM and Today

To make a meaningful comparison between the PETM and today, Ridgwell and Schmidt built large-scale simulations of the ocean at both points of time. They created a virtual version of the Earth 55 million years ago and let the simulation run until it reached a stable state. The pH level of their simulated ocean fell within the range of estimates of the pH of the actual ocean 55 millions years ago. They then built a version of the modern Earth, with today's arrangements of continents, average temperature, and other variables. They let the modern world reach a stable state and then checked the pH of the ocean. Once again, it matched the real pH found in the oceans today.

## The Biggest Threat from Human Activity

The biggest threat from human activity is in increased carbon dioxide emissions causing increased acidity in the oceans. As the amount of atmospheric carbon dioxide increases, more of it reacts chemically with sea water, producing ions (electrically-charged atoms or groups of atoms) of bicarbonate and hydrogen, which increase acidity in water.

*Sher Azad*, Sri Lanka Daily News, *April 19, 2012.*
*www.dailynews.lk.*

Ridgwell and Schmidt then jolted both of these simulated oceans with massive injections of carbon dioxide. They added 6.8 trillion tons of carbon over 10,000 years to their PETM world. Using conservative projections of future carbon emissions, they added 2.1 trillion tons of carbon over just a few centuries to their modern world. Ridgwell and Schmidt then used the model to estimate how easily carbonate would dissolve at different depths of the ocean.

The results were strikingly different. Ridgwell and Schmidt found that ocean acidification is happening about ten times faster today than it did 55 million years ago. And while the saturation horizon rose to 1,500 meters 55 million years ago, it will lurch up to 550 meters on average by 2150, according to the model.

## A New Wave of Extinctions

The PETM was powerful enough to trigger widespread extinctions in the deep oceans. Today's faster, bigger changes to the ocean may well bring a new wave of extinctions. Paleontologists [scientists who study prehistoric life through fossils] haven't found signs of major extinctions of corals or other carbonate-based species in surface waters around PETM. But since today's ocean acidification is so much stronger, it may affect life in shallow water as well. "We can't say things for sure about impacts on ecosystems, but there is a lot of cause for concern," says Ridgwell.

Ellen Thomas, a paleoceanographer at Yale University, says that the new paper "is highly significant to our ideas on ocean acidification." But she points out that life in the ocean was buffeted by more than just a falling pH. "I'm not convinced it's the whole answer," she says. The ocean's temperature rose and oxygen levels dropped. Together, all these changes had complex effects on the ocean's biology 55 million years ago. Scientists now have to determine what sort of combined effect they will have on the ocean in the future.

Our carbon-fueled civilization is affecting life everywhere on Earth, according to the work of scientists like Ridgwell—even life that dwells thousands of feet underwater. "The reach of our actions can really be quite global," says Ridgwell. It's entirely possible that the ocean sediments that form in the next few centuries will change from the white of calcium carbonate back to red clay, as ocean acidification wipes out deep-sea ecosystems.

"It will give people hundreds of millions of years from now something to identify our civilization by," says Ridgwell.

> *"There is no evidence whatsoever that the oceans have become 'more acidic.' The oceans are in fact pronouncedly alkaline, and will remain so however much $CO_2$ we add to the atmosphere."*

# Claims About Ocean Acidification Are Overblown and Scientifically Baseless

*Christopher Monckton*

*Christopher Monckton is a former adviser to former British prime minister Maragret Thatcher and a self-proclaimed climate change skeptic. In the following viewpoint, he argues that there is no evidence that increased human-made carbon dioxide ($CO_2$) levels in the atmosphere have more than a negligible effect on the $CO_2$ levels in the ocean and that human-made $CO_2$ is not responsible for any claimed ocean acidification. Therefore it follows, Monckton contends, that human-made $CO_2$ is also not responsible for a claimed decrease in ocean nutrients. The increase in acidification must be attributed to different, likely natural causes, Monckton concludes.*

As you read, consider the following questions:

1. According to the author, how much $CO_2$ can be found in the oceans compared to the atmosphere?

2. According to Monckton, what tends to facilitate calcification?

3. In the author's opinion, what effect will global warming have on seawater and thus on its acidity?

In April 2010, a sea-fisherman gave testimony about ocean "acidification" before the US Senate. The list of supposed effects of ocean "acidification" included in the fisherman's testimony seems to have been written for him by climate-extremist lobbyists. His items are in *italics*; replies are in Roman [type]face.

> *Research shows that $CO_2$ emissions from burning of fossil fuels and other manmade sources of $CO_2$ are absorbed into the ocean from the atmosphere. In the ocean, the $CO_2$ reacts to form carbonic acid. The acid changes the ocean's chemistry.*

$CO_2$ from whatever source, natural or manmade, is exchanged between the atmosphere and the ocean. Some 30% of all manmade $CO_2$ emissions can be expected to accumulate in the oceans. However, *the oceans already contain 70 times as much $CO_2$ as the atmosphere.* If, therefore, we were to double the $CO_2$ concentration in the atmosphere, an additional partial pressure equivalent to just 30% of today's atmospheric concentration would end up in the oceans—an increase amounting to less than 0.48% of what is already there. That would simply not be enough, on any view, to cause any appreciable "acidification" of the oceans.

## No Evidence of Ocean Acidification

> *Ocean acidification is real. It has been documented by researchers all over the world and there is no doubt that the pH of the ocean is dropping, becoming more acidic.*

There is no evidence whatsoever that the oceans have become "more acidic". The oceans are in fact pronouncedly alkaline, and will remain so however much $CO_2$ we add to the atmosphere. The pH or acid-base index is neutral at a value of 7; acid below 7; alkaline (also known as "base") above 7. The oceans are currently at a pH of 7.9–8.2. No serious scientist suggests that the oceans will become acid: at worst, they will come a little closer to neutrality. To put this in context, ordinary rainwater is acid, with a pH of 5.2.

There is not the slightest danger that the oceans will become acid at all, let alone as acid as harmless rainwater. The reason is that the oceans run over rocks, which react chemically with seawater to keep it firmly alkaline.

Nor is it at all clear that "the pH of the ocean is dropping". At most, the pH may have fallen by 0.1 acid-base units over the past century, but we do not know for sure because no comprehensive, worldwide measurements have ever been taken by a single research project, and there were certainly far too few measurements a century ago to provide a reliable baseline from which any such conclusion can be drawn.

## $CO_2$ Cannot Be the Reason

What is certain is that even a shift of as little as 0.1 acid-base units cannot have been caused by the change in $CO_2$ concentration, because in the past 250 years we have added only 0.19% to the partial pressure of $CO_2$ already pre-existing in the oceans. This is too little to make any measurable difference to the acid-base balance of the oceans.

*Measurements show that the open ocean, on average, is about 30% more acidic today than it was before the Industrial Revolution. In some places, like the West coast, local factors compound that change in seawater. With upwelling or the kind of conditions that produce nutrient-driven hypoxia like we get in the Gulf of Mexico, seawater can become corrosive to some of the fish and shellfish and to the species they eat.*

## Ocean Changes Pose No Threat

Some parts of the ocean are already experiencing conditions that were not forecast to arrive until 2100 . . . and are doing so with no ill effects.

As a result, I'm not particularly concerned about a small change in oceanic pH from the change in atmospheric $CO_2$. The ocean will adapt, some creatures' ranges will change a bit, some species will be slightly advantaged and others slightly disadvantaged.

*Willis Eschenbach,*
*Watts Up with That?, December 27, 2011.*
*http://wattsupwiththat.com.*

Unfortunately, there were too few measurements 250 years ago to allow any such conclusion to be drawn. While it is true that a movement of 0.1 acid-base units towards neutrality would increase the partial pressure of hydrogen ions (the pH) in seawater by some 30%, it is by no means certain that such a movement has actually occurred: measurements in the past were simply not frequent enough or adequate enough.

Besides, even if there has been a movement of 0.1 acid-base units towards neutrality, it is blindingly obvious that the minuscule increase of <0.2% in the partial pressure of $CO_2$ in the oceans for which humankind is responsible cannot have been more than an altogether insignificant contributor.

$CO_2$ is in fact only the seventh on the list of substances whose partial pressures in seawater might in theory influence its acid-base balance. Therefore, if there has been a small movement towards neutrality in the oceans, some other cause than $CO_2$ must be looked for.

## CO$_2$ Does Not Decrease Nutrients

*Mixing CO$_2$ into seawater doesn't just make it more acidic. The carbonic acid from CO$_2$ changes a lot of the ocean's chemistry. For one thing, it reduces the availability of nutrients in seawater that clams, oysters, crabs, lobsters, corals need to build and maintain their shells and skeletons. They absorb nutrients from the seawater. The increased acidity depletes those nutrients. That makes it harder (and sometimes impossible) for a lot of these shell-builders to survive.*

Since there has been no increased acidity, the argument that the insignificant additional partial pressure of CO$_2$ in the oceans that could in theory be attributed to humankind is reducing "the availability of nutrients" is without foundation. Likewise, <0.2% additional CO$_2$ in the oceans (i.e. less than a one-in-500 increase in the partial pressure of CO$_2$) is simply not enough to "change a lot of the ocean's chemistry".

Also, additional CO$_2$, combined with the superabundance of calcium ions in the oceans, tends to facilitate calcification, not to inhibit it.

In most regions, there has been no decline in calcification: in those regions where a decline has been noted, the decline cannot have been caused by the barely-measurable increase in the partial pressure of CO$_2$, and must have been caused by something else (such as changes in the activity of the 220,000 subsea volcanoes that are known to exist).

## The Increase of CO$_2$ Is Natural

*Even small changes in the ocean's chemistry can disrupt the marine food web and cause trouble for fish higher in [the] feeding order. For fishermen to make a living, we need fish stocks that are abundant and dense enough so we can harvest them efficiently.*

The increase of 0.2% in the partial pressure of CO$_2$ in the oceans that may have occurred over the past 250 years is very well within natural variability.

In the Neoproterozoic [1 billion to 543 million years ago] era, for instance, there was 300,000 ppmv [parts per million by volume] $CO_2$ in the atmosphere, some 773 times today's concentration: yet the early oceanic life that led to today's creatures survived.

In the Cambrian era, 550 million years ago, much of the $CO_2$ in the oceans had precipitated out by reaction with magnesium and calcium ions to form dolomitic rock (which contains 40% $CO_2$ from the oceans), and the atmospheric concentration of $CO_2$ had fallen to 7000 ppmv, or 18 times today's concentration: yet it was at that time that the calcite corals first came into existence.

By the Jurassic era, 175 million years ago, atmospheric $CO_2$ concentration was still around 6000 ppmv, more than 15 times today's concentration: yet that was when the delicate aragonite corals first came into existence.

Corals have survived for hundreds of millions of years, and it is nonsense to suggest that a barely-detectable increase in the oceanic partial pressure of $CO_2$ could possibly put them in any way at risk.

As for other calcifying (i.e. shell-building) organisms, they form their shells in an environment in which they topically and biogenically regulate the pH of the water, so that the process of calcification is to a significant extent independent of the pH of the surrounding seawater.

## Global Warming Reverses Acidification

*Cold water absorbs more $CO_2$ than warm water. The oceans in high latitude places like Alaska are more acidic than the warmer waters nearer the equator.*

For reasons explained earlier, no oceans anywhere in the world are "acidic". It is of course true, by Henry's Law [William Henry (1774–1836), an English chemist, formulated a law that states that the solubility of a gas in a liquid depends on the pressure of the gas], that colder oceans will tend to be less alkaline than warmer oceans: however, the official theory is that "global warming" will cause a significant increase in global sea temperatures.

By Henry's Law, the predicted warming of the oceans would cause them to outgas $CO_2$, compensating at least in part for the (in any event insignificant) increase in the partial pressure of oceanic $CO_2$ arising from greater atmospheric concentration. This is particularly true in the polar oceans, which have warmed more, on average, than the oceans as a whole.

## A $CO_2$ Increase Does Not Harm Marine Life

*For a lot of species, it looks like they are most vulnerable in early life, especially their larval stages.*

Even if a few species are vulnerable to a small reduction in the alkalinity of the oceans, and even if there has been a reduction in the alkalinity of the oceans, since $CO_2$ cannot be the cause of the reduction in alkalinity it is not and will not be harmful to the species in question.

*Even adult shellfish, corals and other calcifiers show slower rates of shell building, diminished reproduction, muscle wastage, and other problems when exposed to acidified seawater.*

Laboratory experiments in which hydrochloric acid is added to seawater to simulate "acidification" of the oceans do indeed cause the effects described: however, the addition of hydrochloric acid (in the absence of balancing stoicheia [factors] that are nearly always omitted in such experiments) drives the chemical reaction in the opposite direction to the addition of $CO_2$.

No laboratory experiment in which as little as 0.2% additional $CO_2$ is added to seawater has been conducted, because it is obvious to all serious researchers that so little an additional partial pressure would simply make virtually no detectable difference to marine organisms. Laboratory experiments in which >0.5% $CO_2$ is added to seawater are simply unrealistic, because humankind's activities, even in a century, will not add more than 0.5% to the existing partial pressure of $CO_2$ in the oceans.

The notion that past or foreseeable manmade emissions of $CO_2$ and consequent increases in $CO_2$ concentration in the atmosphere will raise the partial pressure of $CO_2$ in the oceans enough to make any measurable difference to their acid-base balance is without scientific foundation. If there has been a global decline in oceanic pH, the decline has been small, and cannot be attributed chiefly (or, in effect, at all) to manmade $CO_2$ emissions. Other causes, probably natural, must be looked for.

> *"Offshore oil and gas drilling poses serious risks to the environmental and economic health of our ocean resources."*

# Offshore Oil Drilling Endangers Oceans

*Natural Resources Defense Council*

*The Natural Resources Defense Council (NRDC) is an environmental protection group. In the following viewpoint, the group argues that offshore drilling is dangerous to the environment, as proven by the hundreds of leaks and spills in the wake of natural disasters such as Hurricanes Ike and Katrina. The 1989* Exxon Valdez *disaster has shown, according to the NRDC, that oil spills cause financial losses to coastal communities, as well as lasting ecological damage. Even routine drilling causes pollution and harms marine life, the NRDC asserts. The group concludes that because increased offshore drilling will not lower the cost of oil, allowing offshore drilling in protected areas has no benefits.*

As you read, consider the following questions:

1. According to the NRDC, how many oil spills were caused by Hurricanes Katrina and Rita combined?

2. What is "produced water," according to the author?

3. According to the NRDC, how does offshore drilling affect the price of oil?

Healthy oceans are critically important to marine life and to coastal communities whose economies rely on tourism and fishing. Opening up new offshore areas to drilling risks permanent damage to our oceans and beaches without reducing our dependence on oil. When oil spills occur they can bring catastrophic harm to marine life and devastating losses for local businesses. Even routine exploration and drilling activities bring harm to many marine species. The Administration and Congress must work together to assess the environmental impacts of offshore drilling before making key decisions about offshore oil and gas activities in new areas or Alaska.

## Serious Environmental Risks

Expanded offshore drilling poses the risk of oil spills ruining our beaches from Florida to Maine and along the Pacific Coast, bringing harm to those who live, work, and vacation along the coasts, as well as harming habitats critical to plants and animals.

Oil spills can quickly traverse vast distances. For example, when powered by the Gulf of Mexico's Loop Current, an oil spill in the eastern Gulf of Mexico could affect Florida's Panhandle beaches and even travel around the Florida Keys to wreak havoc on estuaries and beaches from the Everglades to Cape Canaveral. Contamination from the massive 1989 *Exxon Valdez* oil spill [in Prince William Sound, Alaska, on March 24, 1989,] reached shorelines nearly 600 miles away; if the spill had occurred on the East Coast, it would have extended from Massachusetts to North Carolina.

In September 2008, Hurricane Ike destroyed oil platforms, tanks, and pipelines throughout the Gulf of Mexico, releasing at least a half-million gallons of crude oil. During Hurricanes Katrina [2005] and Rita [2005] there were 125 spills from platforms, rigs, and pipelines on the ocean's Outer Continental Shelf, releasing almost 685,000 gallons of petroleum products. Worse yet, if you include the land-based infrastructure that supports offshore drilling, the damage from these two hurricanes includes 595 spills releasing millions of gallons of oil.

## Exacting a Serious Toll

Oil spills exact a serious toll on coastal economies, including our approximately $35 billion commercial fishing and $60 billion ocean and coastal tourism and recreation industries. The damage and clean up costs following the *Exxon Valdez* spill were so extensive that Exxon paid out more than one billion dollars to the federal and state governments for damages and clean up costs—and still [as of 2009] owes fishermen, Alaska Natives, business owners, and others a billion dollars to redress the spill's harm.

In another example of economic and environmental damage, a July 2008 accident between a chemical tanker and an oil barge discharged more than 270,000 gallons of fuel oil, closing a huge swath of the Lower Mississippi River to vessel traffic for several days. The Port of New Orleans, located at the center of the world's busiest port complex, was shut down and residents were asked to conserve water when water intakes were closed to prevent contamination of drinking water.

## Lasting Ecological Impacts

According to the National Academy of Sciences, current cleanup methods can only remove a small fraction of the oil spilled into the ocean, leaving the remaining oil to continue affecting ocean ecosystems over time. Scientists investigating the long-term impacts of the *Exxon Valdez* spill estimate that nearly 20,000 gallons of oil from that spill remain in Prince

William Sound, continuing to harm threatened and endangered species and undermine their recovery. Marine mammals, sea birds, fish, shellfish, and other sea life are extremely vulnerable to oil pollution and the long-term toxic effects can impair reproductive success for generations. Studies have shown that tiny amounts of oil—as little as one part per billion—can harm pink salmon and cause their eggs to fail.

## Oil Drilling Creates Pollution

In addition to environmental damage from oil spills, the routine operations associated with offshore drilling produce many toxic wastes and other forms of pollution. For example, each drill well generates tens of thousands of gallons of waste drilling muds (materials used to lubricate drill bits and maintain pressure) and cuttings. Drilling muds contain toxic metals such as mercury, lead, and cadmium that may bioaccumulate and biomagnify in marine organisms, including in our seafood supply.

The water that is brought up from a given well along with oil and gas, referred to as "produced water," contains its own toxic brew of benzene, arsenic, lead, toluene, and varying amounts of radioactive pollutants. Each oil platform can discharge hundreds of thousands of gallons of this produced water daily, contaminating both local waters and those down current from the discharge. An average oil and gas exploration well spews roughly 50 tons of nitrogen oxides, 13 tons of carbon monoxide, 6 tons of sulfur oxides, and 5 tons of volatile organic chemicals.

## Oil Exploration Harms Marine Life

Seismic surveys designed to estimate the size of an oil and gas reserve generate their own environmental problems. To carry out such surveys, ships tow multiple airgun arrays that emit thousands of high-decibel explosive impulses to map the seafloor. The auditory assault from seismic surveys has been found to damage or kill fish eggs and larvae and to impair the hearing and health of fish, making them vulnerable to predators and leaving them unable to locate prey or mates or communicate with each other. These disturbances disrupt and displace important migratory patterns, pushing marine life away from suitable habitats like nurseries and foraging, mating, spawning, and migratory corridors. In addition, seismic surveys have been implicated in whale beaching and stranding incidents.

Offshore drilling requires the construction of significant onshore infrastructure such as new roads, pipelines, and processing facilities, which are often built on formerly pristine beaches. Thanks in part to drilling operations, Louisiana is losing roughly 24 square miles of coastal wetlands each year, eating away at natural storm barriers and increasing the risks of storm damage, including damage from oil spills.

## No Significant Impact on Prices

According to the Department of Energy's Energy Information Administration, drilling in areas previously closed to oil and gas drilling by Presidential and Congressional actions "would not have a significant impact on domestic crude oil and natural gas production . . . before 2030 [the end of the analysis period]." Even then, "Because oil prices are determined on the international market . . . any impact on average wellhead prices is expected to be insignificant."

Offshore drilling will not lower energy costs, reduce our dependence on foreign oil, or create millions of new jobs the way that investing in clean renewable energy will. Rather than trying to drill our way out of this problem, we must act now to become less dependent on oil and increase our supply of renewable and sustainable energy sources.

## Recommendations for Managing Offshore Resources

Offshore oil and gas drilling poses serious risks to the environmental and economic health of our ocean resources and coastal communities. If the [Barack Obama] Administration continues to consider offshore drilling, it is critical that we fully consider these impacts before opening up any new areas to drilling. We also should suspend new leasing and any drilling and seismic activities on existing leases in the Beaufort and Chukchi Seas [in the Arctic Ocean around Alaska] until we have the necessary information to make sensible energy policy decisions.

The Administration should work with Congress to request the following:

*An assessment from the National Academy of Sciences (NAS) of the impact that offshore oil and gas leasing would have on coastal and ocean ecosystems, taking into account the other stressors these ecosystems are already facing.*

It is important that the independent NAS review consider all relevant information, including from academic scientists, coastal states, and natural resource agencies such as the National Oceanic and Atmospheric Administration, in addition to data that exists within the Department of the Interior.

*An assessment by the Government Accounting Office of the impacts on OCS [outer continental shelf] leasing and development on the price and supply of oil and gas.*

The Administration should not open up new offshore lands to oil and gas drilling until the findings of these assessments are available. In the Beaufort and Chukchi Seas, there should be a "time out" on all oil and gas activities until an Arctic conservation and development plan is prepared by a presidentially appointed interagency task force.

> *"[There is] 50 times more marine life around an oil production platform than in the surrounding Gulf [of Mexico] bottoms."*

# Offshore Oil Drilling Poses No Danger to Oceans

*Humberto Fontova*

*Humberto Fontova is an author, columnist, and public speaker. In the following viewpoint, Fontova compares Louisiana, where offshore drilling is allowed, to Florida, where it is prohibited, and concludes that the transportation of oil is more hazardous than oil production. Therefore, Fontova argues, banning drilling for fear of oil spills creates an unnecessary energy dependency on other nations. He cites studies that show that ocean life has flourished around oil rigs, which proves that offshore drilling may have environmental benefits, while urban runoff and sewage is dangerous to marine life. The Louisiana Rigs to Reef program turns unused rigs into artificial reefs, Fontova explains, increasing overall ocean health.*

As you read, consider the following questions:

1. As noted by Fontova, what is Louisiana's percentage of fisheries and what is its percentage of oil production?

2. According to the author, what is the reason for banning offshore drilling?

3. What, according to Fontova, is considered a sign of health for reefs?

Louisiana produces almost 30 per cent of America's commercial fisheries. Only Alaska (ten times the size of the Bayou state) produces slightly more. So obviously, Louisiana's coastal waters are immensely rich and prolific in seafood.

These same coastal waters contain 3,200 of the roughly 3,700 offshore production platforms in the Gulf of Mexico. From these, Louisiana also produces 25 per cent of America's domestic oil, and no major oil spill has ever soiled its coast. So for those interested in evidence over hysterics, by simply looking bayou-ward, a lesson in the "environmental perils" of offshore oil drilling presents itself very clearly.

## Offshore Drilling Is Safe

Fashionable Florida, on the other hand, which zealously prohibits offshore oil drilling, had its gorgeous "Emerald Coast" panhandle beaches soiled by an ugly oil spill in 1976. This spill, as almost all oil spills, resulted from the transportation of oil—not from the extraction of oil. Assuming such as Hugo Chavez [president of Venezuela, 1999–2013] deign to keep selling us oil, we'll need increasingly more and we'll need to keep transporting it stateside—typically to refineries in Louisiana and Texas.

This path takes those tankers (as the one in 1976) smack in front of Florida's panhandle beaches. Recall the [*Exxon*] *Valdez* [which ran aground in Prince William Sound, Alaska, on March 4, 1989], the [*Amoco*] *Cadiz*, [which ran aground at the coast of Brittany, France, on March 16, 1978], the *Argo Merchant* [which ran aground on Nantucket Island, Massachusetts, on December 15, 1976]. These were all tanker spills. The production of oil is relatively clean and safe. Again, it's the transportation that presents the greatest risk. And even these spills (though hyped hysterically as environmental catastrophes) always play out as minor blips, those pictures of oil-soaked seagulls notwithstanding. To the horror and anguish of professional greenies, Alaska's Prince William Sound recovered completely. More birds get fried by landing on power lines and smashed to pulp against picture windows in one week than perished from three decades of oil spills.

For fear of oil spills, as of 2008, the U.S. Federal government and various states ban drilling in thousands upon thousands of square miles off the U.S. Coast. These areas, primarily on the Outer Continental Shelf, hold an estimated 115 billion barrels of oil and 633 trillion cubic feet of natural gas. This leaves America's energy needs increasingly at the mercy of foreign autocrats, despots and maniacs. All the while worldwide demand for oil ratchets ever and ever upward.

## Marine Life Thrives Around Rigs

"Environmentalists" wake up in the middle of the night sweating and whimpering about offshore oil platforms only because they've never seen what's under them. This proliferation of marine life around the platforms turned on its head every "environmental expert" opinion of its day.

The original plan, mandated by federal environmental "experts" back in the late '40s, was to remove the big, ugly, polluting, environmentally hazardous contraptions as soon as they stopped producing. Fine, said the oil companies.

About 15 years ago some wells played out off Louisiana and the oil companies tried to comply. Their ears are still ringing from the clamor fishermen put up. Turns out those platforms are going nowhere, and by popular demand of those with a bigger stake in the marine environment than any "environmentalist."

Every "environmental" superstition against these structures was turned on its head. Marine life had EXPLODED around these huge artificial reefs: A study by LSU's [Louisiana State University's] Sea Grant college shows that 85 percent of Louisiana fishing trips involve fishing around these platforms. The same study shows 50 times more marine life around an oil production platform than in the surrounding Gulf bottoms.

## Urban Runoff Exceeds Rig Spills

An environmental study (by apparently honest scientists) revealed that urban runoff and treated sewage dump 12 times the amount of petroleum into the Gulf than those thousands of oil production platforms. And oil seeping naturally through the ocean floor into the Gulf, where it dissipates over time, accounts for 7 times the amount spilled by rigs and pipelines in any given year.

The Flower Garden coral reefs lie off the Louisiana-Texas border. Unlike any of the Florida Keys reefs, they're surrounded by dozens of offshore oil platforms.

These have been pumping away for the past 50 years. Yet according to G.P. Schmahl, a Federal biologist who worked for decades in both places, "The Flower Gardens are much healthier, more pristine than anything in the Florida Keys. It was a surprise to me," he admits. "And I think it's a surprise to most people."

## The Rigs to Reef Program

"A key measure of the health of a reef is the amount of area taken up by coral," according to a report by Steve Gittings, the National Oceanic and Atmospheric Administration's science coordinator for marine sanctuaries. "Louisiana's Flower Garden boasts nearly 50 percent coral cover. In the Florida Keys it can run as little as 5 percent."

Mark Ferrulo, a Florida "environmental activist" uses the very example of Louisiana for his anti-offshore drilling campaign, calling Louisiana's coast "the nation's toilet."

Florida's fishing fleet must love fishing in toilets, and her restaurants serving what's in them. Most of the red snapper you eat in Florida restaurants are caught around Louisiana's oil platforms. We see the Florida-registered boats tied up to them constantly. Sometimes us locals can barely squeeze in.

In 1986 Louisiana started the Rigs to Reef program, a co-operative effort by oil companies, the feds and the state. This program literally pays the oil companies to keep the platforms in the Gulf. Now some platforms are simply cut off at the bottom and toppled over as artificial reefs; over 60 have been toppled thus far.

A few years back, Louisiana Wildlife and Fisheries officials were invited to Australia to help them with a similar program. Think about it: here's Australia, the nation with the Great Barrier Reef, the world's biggest natural reef, the world's top dive destination—they're asking help from "the nation's toilet" about developing exciting dive sites by using the very structures that epitomize (in greenie eyes) environmental disaster.

America desperately needs more domestic oil. In the process of producing it, we'd also get dynamite fishing, dynamite diving, and a cheaper tab for broiled red snapper with shrimp topping.

> *"Claims that the 'Great Garbage Patch' between California and Japan is twice the size of Texas are grossly exaggerated."*

# The Extent of the Great Pacific Garbage Patch Has Been Grossly Exaggerated

## Oregon State University News and Research Communications

*The Oregon State University College of Earth, Oceanic, and Atmospheric Sciences (CEOAS) is internationally recognized as a leader in the study of the earth as an integrated system. In the following viewpoint, the CEOAS claims that alarmist voices have misrepresented the size of a swath of plastic trash in the Pacific Ocean known as the Great Garbage Patch. According to the author, the garbage patch has not grown since the 1980s, despite greater production and consumption of plastics. Removing the plastic patch would be difficult and costly, the CEOAS asserts, and would endanger microorganisms and marine life caught in the cleanup effort. The author grants that although some micro-*

*organisms thrive on plastic, the ocean should not be used as a junkyard and concludes that any sensible dialogue should focus on ways to prevent the increase of plastic debris.*

As you read, consider the following questions:

1. According to the author, how big is the Great Pacific Garbage Patch compared to the state of Texas?

2. According to the CEOAS, what is "the heartbeat of the ocean"?

3. Aside from the ocean's surface, where else does the author claim debris collects?

There is a lot of plastic trash floating in the Pacific Ocean, but claims that the "Great Garbage Patch" between California and Japan is twice the size of Texas are grossly exaggerated, according to an analysis by an Oregon State University scientist.

Further claims that the oceans are filled with more plastic than plankton, and that the patch has been growing tenfold each decade since the 1950s are equally misleading, pointed out Angelicque "Angel" White, an assistant professor of oceanography at Oregon State.

"There is no doubt that the amount of plastic in the world's oceans is troubling, but this kind of exaggeration undermines the credibility of scientists," White said. "We have data that allow us to make reasonable estimates; we don't need the hyperbole [exaggeration]. Given the observed concentration of plastic in the North Pacific, it is simply inaccurate to state that plastic outweighs plankton, or that we have observed an exponential increase in plastic."

White has pored over published literature and participated in one of the few expeditions solely aimed at understanding the abundance of plastic debris and the associated impact of plastic on microbial communities. That expedition was part of research funded by the National Science Foundation through C-MORE, the Center for Microbial Oceanography: Research and Education.

The studies have shown that if you look at the actual area of the plastic itself, rather than the entire North Pacific subtropical gyre [opposing ocean currents that create a whirlpool], the hypothetically "cohesive" plastic patch is actually less than 1 percent of the geographic size of Texas.

"The amount of plastic out there isn't trivial," White said. "But using the highest concentrations ever reported by scientists produces a patch that is a small fraction of the state of Texas, not twice the size."

Another way to look at it, White said, is to compare the amount of plastic found to the amount of water in which it was found. "If we were to filter the surface area of the ocean equivalent to a football field in waters having the highest concentration (of plastic) ever recorded," she said, "the amount of plastic recovered would not even extend to the 1-inch line."

## No Increase in Plastic Debris

Recent research by scientists at the Woods Hole Oceanographic Institution found that the amount of plastic, at least in the Atlantic Ocean, hasn't increased since the mid-1980s—despite greater production and consumption of materials made from plastic, she pointed out.

"Are we doing a better job of preventing plastics from getting into the ocean?" White said. "Is more plastic sinking out of the surface waters? Or is it being more efficiently broken down? We just don't know. But the data on hand simply do not suggest that 'plastic patches' have increased in size. This is certainly an unexpected conclusion, but it may in part reflect the high spatial and temporal variability of plastic concentrations in the ocean and the limited number of samples that have been collected."

The hyperbole about plastic patches saturating the media rankles White, who says such exaggeration can drive a wedge between the public and the scientific community. One recent claim that the garbage patch is as deep as the Golden Gate Bridge is tall is completely unfounded, she said.

"Most plastics either sink or float," White pointed out. "Plastic isn't likely to be evenly distributed through the top 100 feet of the water column."

## Some Microbes Thrive on Plastic

White says there is growing interest in removing plastic from the ocean, but such efforts will be costly, inefficient, and may have unforeseen consequences. It would be difficult, for example, to "corral" and remove plastic particles from ocean waters without inadvertently removing phytoplankton, zooplankton, and small surface-dwelling aquatic creatures.

"These small organisms are the heartbeat of the ocean," she said. "They are the foundation of healthy ocean food chains and immensely more abundant than plastic debris."

The relationship between microbes and plastic is what drew White and her C-MORE colleagues to their analysis in the first place. During a recent expedition, they discovered that photosynthetic microbes were thriving on many plastic particles, in essence confirming that plastic is prime real estate for certain microbes.

## Plastic Does Not Belong in the Ocean

White also noted that while plastic may be beneficial to some organisms, it can also be toxic. Specifically, it is well-known that plastic debris can adsorb toxins such as PCB [polychlorinated biphenyl].

"On one hand, these plastics may help remove toxins from the water," she said. "On the other hand, these same toxin-laden particles may be ingested by fish and seabirds. Plastic clearly does not belong in the ocean."

Among other findings, which White believes should be part of the public dialogue on ocean trash:

- Calculations show that the amount of energy it would take to remove plastics from the ocean is roughly 250 times the mass of the plastic itself;

- Plastic also covers the ocean floor, particularly offshore of large population centers. A recent survey from the state of California found that 3 percent of the southern California Bight's ocean floor was covered with plastic—roughly half the amount of ocean floor covered by lost fishing gear in the same location. But little, overall, is known about how much plastic has accumulated at the bottom of the ocean, and how far offshore this debris field extends;

- It is a common misperception that you can see or quantify plastic from space. There are no tropical plastic islands out there and, in fact, most of the plastic isn't even visible from the deck of a boat;

- There are areas of the ocean largely unpolluted by plastic. A recent trawl White conducted in a remote section of water between Easter Island and Chile pulled in no plastic at all.

There are other issues with plastic, White said, including the possibility that floating debris may act as a vector for introducing invasive species into sensitive habitats.

## A Call for Preventive Measures

"If there is a takeaway message, it's that we should consider it good news that the 'garbage patch' doesn't seem to be as bad as advertised," White said, "but since it would be prohibitively costly to remove the plastic, we need to focus our efforts on preventing more trash from fouling our oceans in the first place."

# Periodical and Internet Sources Bibliography

*The following articles have been selected to supplement the diverse views presented in this chapter.*

| | |
|---|---|
| David Braun | "Overfishing Leaves Much of the Mediterranean a Dead Sea, Study Finds," *National Geographic*, March 2, 2012. |
| Jan Andries van Franeker | "Plastic Soup on our Plate," Plastic Garbage Project, June 2011. www.plasticgarbageproject.org. |
| Jennifer S. Holland | "The Great Barrier Reef: A Fragile Empire," *National Geographic*, May 2011. |
| Marc Kaufman | "Overfishing Threatening Ocean's Predators," Global Animal, February 28, 2011. www.globalanimal.org. |
| Elizabeth Kolbert | "The Acid Sea," *National Geographic*, April 2011. |
| Mac Margolis | "The Age of Extreme Offshore Oil Is Just Beginning," *Discover*, January 18, 2011. |
| Ocean Conservancy | "Trash Free Seas: It's Time to Stop Trashing Our Ocean," 2012. www.oceanconservancy.org. |
| Wayne Parry | "Could Dumping Iron in the Oceans Slow Global Warming?," *Christian Science Monitor*, July 18, 2012. |
| Science Daily | "One Solution to Overfishing Found," March 19, 2012. www.sciencedaily.com. |
| Tara Thean | "Ocean History Lessons: How Corals Can Protect Themselves from Warming," *Time*, April 3, 2012. |
| Bryan Walsh | "The End of the Line," *Time*, July 7, 2011. |

# CHAPTER 2

# What Ocean Policies Are Best?

# Chapter Preface

In 2004, Victor Smetacek of the Alfred Wegener Institute for Polar and Marine Research in Bremerhaven, Germany, created a bloom of carbon-absorbing algae by sprinkling iron into a naturally encapsulated area of the southern ocean. During the four weeks of the study, more than half the algae died off, sinking into the ocean and taking the carbon they had ingested down into the depths with them. "We were able to track the particles sinking out of the surface layer all the way down to the sediments," says Smetacek. The results of this study were released in 2012, arguing that, in theory, "ironizing" the oceans could speed up the growth of carbon-absorbing algae, which could turn the ocean into a greenhouse-gas-absorbing machine, slowing down the effect of global warming and all the dangers that come with it.

Policy makers, investors, economists, and ecologists are taking notice of the geo-engineering possibilities revealed by this study, yet Smetacek himself warns that his study was too isolated to predict whether a larger scale ironization would indeed have the intended effect. Greenpeace goes a step further, arguing that dumping iron into the ocean on any scale, however large or small, amounts to pollution. "If we're going to be pursuing this as a climate mitigation strategy, then we're looking at a state of the world where we rely on manipulating the ocean on a truly huge scale and that would undoubtedly have large and possibly irreversible effects on ocean ecosystems," says David Santillo, a Greenpeace scientist. In other words, counteracting global warming, which has been and will keep changing our ecosystem, with geo-engineered fixes that will change the ecosystem as well, is utterly counterproductive.

Hugh Powell, an environmental issues writer with the Woods Hole Oceanographic Institution warns:

Large-scale iron fertilization, in altering the base of the food chain, might lead to undesirable changes in fish stocks and whale populations. Increased decomposition of sinking organic matter could deprive deep waters of oxygen or produce other greenhouse gases more potent than carbon dioxide, such as nitrous oxide and methane. The plankton-choked surface waters could block sunlight needed by deeper corals, or warm the surface layer and change circulation patterns

Opponents to ocean ironization further claim that only a fraction of the carbon drawn by the algae sinks to the bottom, while most remains in the mid-layers of the ocean. Yet, proponents of such geo-engineered algae blooms counter that even that small fraction of carbon absorption may buy enough time to search and find better strategies to combat global warming.

Geo-engineering policies such as ocean ironization are subject to controversy, as any far-reaching policy will have lasting effects—on the environment, on the economy, and on humankind. The viewpoints in the following chapter debate the potential effects of ocean-saving strategies such as marine protected areas, the Clean Water Act, the Ocean Health Index, and the National Ocean Policy.

| *"The [National Ocean Policy] will improve scientific management and will help safeguard the commercial and recreational fishing industries—some of the most fundamental drivers of our ocean economy."*

# The National Ocean Policy Benefits Businesses

## Michael Conathan

*Michael Conathan is director of ocean policy at the Center for American Progress. In the following viewpoint, Conathan argues that the criticism of US president Barack Obama's National Ocean Policy is only partisan rhetoric. He claims that the policy is not federal top-down bureaucracy, because it incorporates regional plans. He further explains that the policy does not overreach by imposing regulations for freshwater bodies, because freshwater and seawater are interrelated with rivers flowing into the ocean. Finally, he argues that the policy encourages and facilitates interagency collaboration.*

As you read, consider the following questions:

1. According to the author, where is President Obama's National Ocean Policy discussed?

2. According to Conathan, what causes the concern of fishing industry groups and fishery management councils?

3. According to the author, what does the National Ocean Policy plan to research?

Even in the bitterest partisan times, ocean issues tend to exist outside the traditional political boxing ring. They usually foster alliances based far more on geography than on party affiliation. Members who represent coastal states and districts usually recognize the value of sustaining and investing in our valuable ocean resources, and they prioritize them more than their inland counterparts. But in recent months [early 2012] the escalation of rancor and polarization encompassed even the normally temperate issue of ocean policy.

Nowhere is this tone more prevalent than in the House Committee on Natural Resources, where Republicans have made President Barack Obama's National Ocean Policy public enemy number one.

Ever since its roll-out, the policy—implemented by an executive order in 2010 to provide a comprehensive set of guiding principles for the "stewardship of the ocean, our coasts, and the Great Lakes"—has been taking fire from opponents who cite it as an overreach that would spawn "job-killing regulations," according to Rep. Doc Hastings (R-WA) and would mean the "death of all land-use planning" in this country, in the words of Rep. Tom McClintock (R-CA).

Leaving aside the inherent contradiction espoused by Rep. McClintock—that the National Ocean Policy's nefarious efforts to develop a framework for the great evil of ocean-use planning would in turn kill the wonderful benefits of land-use planning—boiling these statements down to their roots leaves little more than bald political rhetoric. In practice, the policy will improve scientific management and will help safeguard the commercial and recreational fishing industries—some of the most fundamental drivers of our ocean economy.

Rep. Hastings, who chairs the Committee on Natural Resources, and Rep. McClintock both hail from coastal states, yet neither of the regions they represent in Congress actually touch the Pacific Ocean. Still, the rivers that run through their districts ultimately terminate in the sea, and new findings are proving regularly what we already knew—what enters those rivers flushes into the ocean and directly affects all facets of marine life, including our fisheries.

Rep. Hastings has held multiple hearings about the National Ocean Policy in his committee this year [2012], repeatedly questioning administration officials, scientists, industry members, and advocates about what he sees as an authoritarian overreach and a prime example of the regulatory stranglehold the Obama administration is putting on America's economic growth. (I testified before Rep. Hastings's Committee on October 29, 2011.)

On April 2 Rep. Hastings sent a letter to his colleagues in the House Appropriations Committee—the holders of the congressional purse strings—asking them to "prohibit the use of funds for the implementation of the National Ocean Policy."

On the whole, many fishing industry groups, including the regional fishery management councils tasked with developing fishery management plans, have expressed concern over the policy since its inception because they feared their voices would not be heard during the development of specific policy recommendations. Since the initial proposal was announced, the administration has taken steps to alleviate those concerns, including formally incorporating the councils in regional planning efforts.

Despite these improvements, Rep. Hastings has been joined in his effort to defund the policy by a coalition of ocean and inland industry groups, including commercial and recreational fishing organizations. In their letter the groups call out potential benefits of a national ocean policy "designed to stimulate job creation and economic growth while conserving the natu-

## Federal Stewardship of the Oceans

Our valuable ocean and coastal resources are vulnerable to misuse, and need to be thoughtfully managed to ensure they will be healthy and productive for current and future generations.

The Federal Government has a critical role to play as a steward, leading the way in sound management of these ecosystems working with States, Tribes, and other partners to find common solutions to key challenges, and ensuring the Nation's valuable ocean, coastal, and Great Lakes resources continue to provide us with the wealth of benefits that ensure our well-being and prosperity. Recognizing this, the National Policy for the Stewardship of the Ocean, Our Coasts, and the Great Lakes (hereinafter "National Ocean Policy") was established by Executive Order 13547 on July 19, 2010. The National Ocean Policy provides that Federal agencies will "ensure the protection, maintenance, and restoration of the health of ocean, coastal, and Great Lakes ecosystems and resources, enhance the sustainability of ocean and coastal economies, preserve our maritime heritage, support sustainable uses and access, provide for adaptive management to enhance our understanding of and capacity to respond to climate change and ocean acidification, and coordinate with our national security and foreign policy interests." . . .

Fishing, energy, transportation, recreation, security, and other uses will be considered collectively and managed comprehensively and collaboratively.

*Barack Obama,*
*"Draft National Ocean Policy Implementation Plan,"*
*January 12, 2012. www.whitehouse.gov.*

ral resources and marine habitat of our oceans and coastal regions." Then, in the next sentence, they contradict this desire by calling for a "pause in implementation" of President Obama's ocean policy, which explicitly shares those goals.

In this letter Rep. Hastings also says the policy is "especially alarming" because it "stretches far inland following rivers and their tributaries upstream for hundreds of miles."

But of course it stretches upstream! There is no impermeable layer dividing salt water from fresh. This is a fundamental reason why we need the policy in the first place. In fact, the policy is designed specifically to ensure adequate and efficient coordination between the agencies responsible for inland activities that affect ocean resources and the agencies that oversee the ocean activities themselves.

The news this week [mid-April 2012] provided specific examples of why such coordination is necessary. Pesticide use was found to affect Pacific salmon populations, and ocean acidification was proven to stunt oyster growth. These may seem like obvious conclusions to draw, but they both exemplify the difficulty in differentiating between oceans and lands. Similar to the estuarine [areas where rivers enter the ocean are called *estuaries*] boundary between salt water and fresh (how salty can fresh water be before it becomes seawater?) our jurisdictional boundaries are equally nebulous.

President Obama famously (if incorrectly) noted this blurring of the lines during his 2011 State of the Union address when he famously poked fun at the government's management of salmon. "The Interior Department handles salmon when they're in freshwater, but the Commerce Department handles them in saltwater. And I hear it gets even more complicated once they're smoked," he quipped to polite laughter in the House chamber and rolling echoes of punditry in the days after the speech.

The reality of salmon management is far more sensible. The Commerce Department's National Oceanic and Atmospheric Administration is actually responsible for salmon species management throughout their range, though the Department of the Interior's Fish and Wildlife Service does manage some salmon habitat programs.

Yet the point remains that what happens upstream in salmon runs can have a dramatic effect on the survival of one of the most valuable fisheries in the country. Thus it makes a great deal of sense that we should coordinate efforts across federal agencies to manage issues that transcend traditional boundaries. For example: If pesticides make life more difficult for salmon, then the pesticide regulators should be talking to the fisheries biologists to figure out how to minimize that impact. This is precisely the kind of interagency collaboration the National Ocean Policy is designed to facilitate.

Further, Hastings's efforts to defund the policy's recommendations not only would prevent government operations from becoming more efficient by collaborating across traditional agency boundaries but could also have devastating ramifications for the day-to-day programs that improve fishery management and make life better for fishermen.

Cutting funding as Rep. Hastings has requested risks eliminating funding for many of the National Oceanic and Atmospheric Administration's existing programs that fishermen rely on or that could greatly enhance the understanding of what factors other than fishing pressure are causing fish stocks to decline and prevent their rebuilding.

Specifically, the National Ocean Policy's Draft Implementation Plan calls for:

- Sustaining ocean observing systems that provide critical data for fishery stock assessments

- Conducting research on what stressors (habitat degradation, pollution, global climate change, etc.) affect fish stocks other than fishing mortality

- Prioritizing a National Shellfish Initiative to investigate potential ecosystem and economic benefits of shellfish aquaculture

- Identifying key ecosystem protection areas to enhance the quality of habitat that provides sanctuary and nurseries for the "more than half of all fish caught in US waters [that] depend on the estuaries and coastal wetlands at some point in their life cycles"

- Understanding and combatting hypoxia (lack of oxygen) caused by polluted runoff from rivers and streams that can lead to massive fish kills, harmful algal blooms, and other phenomena that adversely affect fish populations

These programs are not new, and administration officials have been abundantly clear in their testimony before Congress and, in some cases, in the face of withering interrogation, that the National Ocean Policy does not create any new regulations for how we use our ocean space.

Healthy oceans and coasts are among the strongest economic drivers and most valuable resources our nation possesses. The National Ocean Policy recognizes this fact and sets forth a proactive framework to streamline government involvement, eliminate duplication of effort, and ensure taxpayers get more value for their dollars—exactly what small government Republicans claim they want.

> *"The Obama administration is trying to impose top-down bureaucratic regulation on the use of the oceans and the nation's fisheries, which . . . will put fishing jobs at stake."*

# The National Ocean Policy Endangers Businesses

## Pete Winn

*Pete Winn is a senior editor and writer for CNS News. In the following viewpoint he argues that the National Ocean Policy endangers businesses. Winn cites the Seafood Coalition, which holds that the top-down bureaucracy of the national policy unnecessarily restricts commercial fishing with regulations that have been created by government agencies that are too far removed from the day-to day-operations of the seafood industry and fishery management. In addition, Winn explains, the Seafood Coalition fears that the new policy hinders successful existing programs by diverting their funds.*

As you read, consider the following questions:

1. As noted by the author, how did the Seafood Coalition make its criticism of the National Ocean Policy known?

2. According to Winn, who is heading the National Oceans Council?

3. According to the author, how many domestic fisheries have stopped overfishing?

The nation's commercial fishermen say the [Barack] Obama administration is trying to impose top-down bureaucratic regulation on the use of the oceans and the nation's fisheries, which they say will put fishing jobs at stake.

A group calling itself the Seafood Coalition is calling on Congress to do what it can to scuttle President Obama's National Ocean Policy [NOP], which the president unilaterally imposed by executive order in 2010.

In a letter to the House Natural Resources Committee, the Seafood Coalition said that the president's plan adds a needless level of top-down bureaucracy and regulation on fisheries.

## The Policy Restricts Ocean Use

"The National Ocean Policy creates a federal ocean zoning regime that will likely result in substantial new regulations and restrictions on ocean users," Nils Stolpe, spokesman for the Seafood Coalition, told CNSNews.com on Monday.

The coalition says it is also concerned that the administration is going to take money away from programs that are currently working well to pay for the new layer of bureaucracy.

"What we've asked for in our letter to the chairman was for Congress to use whatever funding capacity they have to stop this," Stolpe said.

The Seafood Coalition describes itself as a "broad national coalition of commercial fishing interests, seafood processors, and coastal communities" that includes members from every region of the U.S. and "accounts for about 85 percent of the fish and shellfish products landed annually in the U.S."

In July of 2010, President Obama signed the order establishing a National Policy for the Stewardship of the Ocean, Our Coasts, and the Great Lakes.

The order directs all federal agencies to implement the Final Recommendations of the Interagency Ocean Policy Task Force, which was created by White House Council on Environmental Quality.

The National Ocean Policy identifies nine objectives and outlines a "flexible framework" for how bureaucrats will "effectively address conservation, economic activity, user conflict, and sustainable use of the ocean, our coasts, and the Great Lakes."

One of the key objectives is called "coastal and marine spatial planning (CMSP)"—which the executive order defines as "a comprehensive, adaptive, integrated, ecosystem-based, and transparent spatial planning process, based on sound science, for analyzing current and anticipated uses of ocean, coastal, and Great Lakes areas."

It added: "In practical terms, coastal and marine spatial planning provides a public policy process for society to better determine how the ocean, our coasts, and Great Lakes are sustainably used and protected—now and for future generations."

## The National Oceans Council

But Stolpe and the Seafood Coalition said CMSP essentially means the imposition of top-down federal planning boards to govern ocean use.

"It establishes a number of regional boards that in essence are in charge of what goes on in the oceans of those particular regions—from a fishing perspective, from an energy development perspective, from a transportation perspective, from a recreational use perspective," Stolpe said.

The executive order also creates a National Oceans Council, headed by White House Science Adviser Dr. John Holdren

## Ocean Zoning Threatens Alaska's Economy

President [Barack] Obama's National Ocean Policy calls for a new "ocean zoning" authority headed by 9 Federally-dominated Regional Planning Bodies with the ability to reach as far inland as each deems necessary to protect ocean ecosystem health. The Regional Planning Bodies will have no representation by the people, communities and businesses that will actually be impacted by the regulations and will create zoning plans without any stakeholder input. However, all Federal agencies, the States, and the regulated industries will be bound by the plan.

*Jill Strait,*
*US House of Representatives Natural Resources Committee,*
*April 3, 2012. http://naturalresources.house.gov.*

and Council for Environmental Quality director Nancy Sutley, to oversee overall ocean planning.

No one from the seafood industry will be part of the council, the coalition said.

"These are people far-far removed from the nitty-gritty of fisheries management," Stolpe told CNSNews.com. "I would assume that they are far-far removed from the nitty-gritty of just about anything."

Stolpe said the regional boards will throw up in the air the bottom-up scheme that has been in effect since 1976, when Congress passed the Magnuson Stevens Fishery Conservation and Management Act to address overfishing.

"The management program we have in place now is working—it's working really well—and we don't need another layer of bureaucracy stuck on top of that," he said.

Stolpe said the commercial seafood industry currently works hand-in-hand with federal and state fisheries managers and scientists to create "an effective management process" which already promotes "sustainable" fishing.

"Eighty percent of our domestic fisheries—fisheries exclusively in the U.S. economic zone—are no longer being overfished," Stolpe said.

The White House, meanwhile, specifically denies the accusation made by the fishing industry.

"The National Ocean Policy in no way restricts any ocean, coastal, or Great Lakes activity, nor does it impose ocean zoning through CMSP or any other component," the White House Web site says.

"Only the Federal agencies are required to follow the regionally developed CMSPs. Tribal, state and local governments will benefit by having a regional CMSP blueprint to follow, and their participation in CMSP is voluntary," the White House added.

## The Policy Diverts Funds

Rep. Don Young (R-Alaska), a member of the House Natural Resources Committee, says he, too, has serious concerns about the administration's National Ocean Policy and feels that Congress should intervene.

Young's office told CNSNews.com that the congressman is pleased that both the House and Senate Commerce appropriations bills defund Coastal and Marine Spatial Planning, but said "it is a real concern" that the National Oceanographic and Atmospheric Agency (NOAA) will simply divert funds from other accounts to make up for these losses.

"Most concerning is that these diversions would more than likely come from existing fisheries management accounts, which is a core emphasis for NOAA and are already underfunded," Young's spokesman, Luke Miller, told CNSNews.com.

"As a result, in the FY 12 [fiscal year 2012] appropriations process, Congressman Young requested that funds be restricted from being used to implement the CMSP program and the Executive Order that created the NOP."

The House Natural Resources Committee has held two hearings on the topic, one of which included CEQ [Council on Environmental Quality] Chairwoman Sutley and NOAA Administrator Dr. Jane Lubchenco.

> "*[Marine] protected areas . . . have a chance of creating a good-quality marine environment that is ecologically adaptable.*"

# Marine Protected Areas Are Essential for Ensuring Ocean Biodiversity

*Chris Maser*

*Chris Maser is a widely published sustainability expert. In the following viewpoint, he explains that the threat to cod in the Gulf of Maine illustrates the need for fishing restrictions in marine protected areas that repair ocean habitats. Maser argues that marine protected areas are designed to protect entire habitats in composition, structure, and function, as opposed to single-species fishery management. Connecting these protected habitats promises sustainable marine biodiversity, Maser asserts. Marine protected areas may bring with them short-term hardships for commercial fishers, Maser concludes, yet short-term solutions will cause long-term harm to the sustainability of biodiversity in the oceans.*

As you read, consider the following questions:

1. According to the author, how many years did it take for Cabo Pulmo National Park to quintuple its biomass?

2. According to Maser, what is the most neglected component of a given habitat?

3. As the author states it, what is the principle upon which marine protected areas are based?

The cod in the Gulf of Maine has been crucial to New England fishermen from Cape Cod to Maine for hundreds of years, and four years ago [in 2008], after a major assessment, it was thought to be one of the region's strongest species. It brought in $15.8 million in 2010, second highest amount behind Georges Bank haddock among the region's 20 regulated bottom-dwelling groundfish.

But data released last year [in 2011] indicated the fish was so severely overfished that even if all fishing on it ended immediately, it wouldn't rebound by 2014 to levels required under federal law.

As a result, fishermen were looking at an 82 percent cut in what they were allowed to catch in 2011, *a catastrophic reduction that would have wiped out fishermen around the region— not just those who rely on cod. That's because major restrictions on cod severely limit fishing on the other key groundfish species, such as flounder and haddock, in order to protect the cod they swim among* (emphasis mine).

From the first indications of cod trouble, fishermen and their advocates have questioned the science behind the new data and Friday [March 30, 2012,] was no exception.

"We don't trust your data," New Hampshire charter boat fisherman Bill Wagner told regulators. "We don't believe there's a shortage of codfish. We don't believe there's a crisis in codfish."

Massachusetts Rep. Ann-Margaret Ferrante, who represents the port of Gloucester, criticized what she characterized as the constant, massive swings in scientific assessments on the size of fish populations.

"We're always in the same dilemma and I don't understand why," she said.

Gloucester fisherman Al Cottone said the new assessment has put the fishing industry "on death row."

"The anxiety the industry feels is unprecedented," he said.

With so much doubt about the science behind the new data, Cottone said, regulators should give fishermen as much fish to catch as possible while they try to remove uncertainties in the numbers.

## The Case of Cabo Pulmo National Park

The above sequence of events is illustrative of the impetus underpinning the concept of marine protected areas, where fishing is excluded as an effective means of repairing complex reef communities, as well as others, while protecting populations of species vulnerable to overfishing. The argument rests on predictions of increases in abundance and size of fishes after the elimination of anthropogenic [human-caused] mortality; in turn, these increases lead to greater production of eggs per area of reef and greater pelagic [open-ocean] dispersal to fishing grounds.

These concepts proved valid in the responses of fish populations to areas closed to fishing in a small Caribbean protected area surrounding the island of Saba in the Netherlands Antilles and in the 44-square-mile Cabo Pulmo National Marine Park, which sits close to where the Gulf [of California, between Baja California and mainland Mexico] opens into the Pacific.

Cabo Pulmo National Park (created in 1995) is the only well-enforced, no-take marine protected area in the Gulf of California, Mexico, primarily because of widespread support from the local community. Within 14 years of Cabo Pulmo closing its borders to fishing, the total biomass of its denizens more than quintupled. Over the same period, the share of top predators, sentinels of a healthy ecosystem, soared also— trends counter to those for fish in unprotected regions of the Gulf. Moreover, the biomass of fish did not change significantly in other protected areas or areas of open access over the same time period.

Nevertheless, the absolute increase in fish biomass at Cabo Pulmo within a decade is the largest measured in a protected area worldwide, and is probably due to a combination of social (strong community leadership, social cohesion, effective enforcement) and ecological factors. The recovery of fish inside Cabo Pulmo has resulted in significant economic benefits, demonstrating that community-managed marine protected areas are a viable solution to non-sustainable coastal development and chronic overfishing.

This strategy is likely to work as intended, however, *only* if networks of stepping-stone-protected-areas are established within a relatively short distance of one another. Within these protected areas, ocean currents form the corridors between and among larger areas of protected habitat throughout the fish community's areas of reproduction, larval transport and settlement, and feeding grounds for adults. That said, planning new protected areas will require serious forethought because the jet stream drives the ocean currents. A shift in the jet stream caused by global warming will affect the location of the various currents and will thus have a potential impact on existing and future networks of protected areas. Before delving too deeply into the idea of protected areas, however, a basic understanding of habitat is necessary.

## Designed to Protect Habitats

As with all terrestrial species, marine species are variously adapted and adaptable to existing and changing configurations of their habitat. Whereas some species are narrowly adapted to a specific set of conditions and thus restricted in both area and flexibility with respect to change, others are broadly adapted and thus more adaptable to pending climate-induced shifts within their oceanic habitats, such as the blue-fin tuna that mingle in and traverse the Atlantic and parts of the Pacific in total disregard to international boundaries.

Most people are at least somewhat familiar with the components of habitat because they, like all terrestrial animals, require: food, water, shelter, space, privacy, and connectivity among them. The same is true in the marine realm, with the exception of fresh water.

Every habitat is based on composition, structure, and function. . . .

To maintain biophysical functions means that we humans must maintain the characteristics of an ecosystem in such a way that its processes are sustainable. The characteristics we must be concerned with are: (1) composition, (2) structure, (3) function, and (4) Nature's disturbance regimes, which periodically alter an ecosystem's composition, structure, and function.

We can, for instance, change the composition of an ecosystem, such as the kinds and arrangement of plants in a forest, grassland, or agricultural corp. This alteration means that composition is malleable to human desire and thus negotiable within the context of cause and effect. In this case, composition is the determiner of the structure and function in that composition is the cause, rather than the effect, of the structure and function.

## Ecosystem Composition and Structure

Composition determines the structure, and structure determines the function. Thus, by negotiating the composition, such as sinking ships in some of the world's oceans during World Wars I and II, we simultaneously negotiate both the structure and function of those particular marine ecosystems. On the other hand, once the composition is in place, the structure and function are set—unless, of course, the composition is altered (the salvage and removal of a sunken ship), at which time both the ecosystem's structure and function are altered accordingly.

In this sense, the composition or kinds of corals and their age classes within a coral reef create a certain structure that is characteristic of the reef at any given age. It is the structure of the reef that creates and maintains certain functions. In turn, it is the composition, structure, and function of a coral reef that determines what kinds animals can live there, how many, and for how long.

Thus, if swimmers wear suntan lotion, which kills part of a coral reef, they change its structure, hence its function, and thus affect the animals. The animals living in and around the reef *are not just a reflection* of its composition at any given point in time. They are ultimately *constrained by it.*

Thus, once the composition is ensconced [set in place], the structure and its attendant functions operate as an interactive unit in terms of the habitat required for the animal(s). In other words, the connectivity—accessibility—of habitat components is particularly important for the resident population, regardless of species, because each habitat has a biological carrying capacity, meaning a finite number of individuals that can live in a particular area without altering it to their detriment.

Nevertheless, people are continually altering the structure and function of this ecosystem or that ecosystem by manipulating its composition—either consciously or *unconsciously, as in overfishing.* Each manipulation has the capacity to change the diversity of species dependent on the structure and function of the resultant habitat. By altering the composition of an ecosystem, people and Nature alter its structure and, in turn, affect how it functions, which in turn determines not only its potential ecosystem services but also what uses humans can derive from those services.

## A Basic Habitat Component

One of the most basic—but neglected—components of a given habitat is its "connectivity," both within a given area and among areas. Human-introduced disturbances, especially fragmentation of habitat, impose stresses with which an ecosystem is ill adapted to cope. Not surprisingly, the *connectivity* of habitats with a seascape is of prime importance to the persistence of plants and animals in viable numbers, which is a matter of biodiversity. In this sense, the seascape must be considered a mosaic of interconnected patches of habitats—stepping stones, if you will—that act as corridors or routes of travel between patches of suitable habitats, such as coral reefs or beds of seagrass.

Seagrasses, which are any one of four submerged, marine, flowering plants, are sometimes termed ecosystem engineers because they create their own habitat by slowing ocean currents. In doing so, they increase sedimentation, which not only gives seagrasses a more nutrient-rich substrate in which to grow but also augments their roots and rhizomes in stabilizing the seabed. Their importance to associated species is due mainly to their three-dimensional structure in the water column, which provides both shelter and vegetated corridors between and among different patches of habitat, such as coral reefs and mangrove islands. Like land plants, seagrasses require sunlight for photosynthesis and thus are limited in their distribution by the clarity of the water in which they grow. In addition, they produce oxygen.

Seagrass serves as habitat for the settlement of larval lobsters and is thus likely associated with the increased abundance of lobsters found in isolated habitats connected by corridors of seagrass. In one study, immigration and emigration of juvenile lobsters were three to four times higher on islands connected by seagrass than on islands surrounded by bare rubble or sand. Rubble fields functioned as barriers to the seafloor dispersal of all but adult lobsters. Hence, the effects of insularity on a population of lobsters could be lessened by surrounding islands with "stepping-stone habitats" in the form of seagrass corridors because they have important functional roles as areas of larval settlement, foraging grounds, or passageways of relative safety through otherwise hostile territory.

Conversely, vegetated corridors can facilitate the access of such predators as the blue crabs to beds of oysters, on which they prey. Accordingly, the spatial proximity of one habitat to another can strongly influence both the population and community dynamics of both. Understanding the trade-off effects of seascape characteristics in estuarine [where freshwater meets seawater] habitats could be useful in predicting the consequences of habitat fragmentation in marine ecosystems, especially where the conservation or repair (or both) of a system is required for the sake of biodiversity and its associated services.

## The Threat of Habitat Fragmentation

Whether populations of plants and animals survive in a particular seascape depends on the rate of local extinctions from a patch of habitat and the rate with which an organism can move among existing patches of habitat. Those species living in habitats isolated as a result of fragmentation—from such things as bottom dredging—are therefore less likely to persist. Fragmentation of habitat, the most serious threat to biological diversity, is the primary cause of the present global crisis in the rate of biological extinctions. In the world's oceans, much, if not most, of the fragmentation of the habitat is a so-called "side effect" of techniques employed in overfishing that increasingly stresses the short-term take of commercial fishes at the long-term expense of the environment. *"Side effect" is an*

## Marine Protected Areas Conserve Biodiversity

The primary ecological objectives of MPAs are to conserve biodiversity and to enhance fishery yields where other forms of fishery management do not work (as may often be the case in developing coastal nations with low institutional capacity for management). In the past, MPAs have typically been small no-take areas ("marine reserves") often implemented at sites with particularly healthy coral reef habitat. Management of these marine reserves involves a ban on harvesting but rarely any regulation of activities occurring outside the reserve (e.g. upland deforestation, road building, etc.). Currently, managers are moving to a paradigm of larger MPA networks implemented within a "ridge to reef" approach to ecosystem-based management, where MPAs, watershed management, and wise land-use practices are included in an integrated coastal management regime.

*World Fish Center, "Lessons Learned and Good Practices in the Management of Coral Reef Marine Protected Areas," www.reefbase.org.*

*economic euphemism. There is no such thing as a side effect— only a direct, but an unintentional effect!*

Modifying the existing connectivity among patches of habitat strongly influences the abundance of species and their patterns of movement. The size, shape, and diversity of patches also influence the patterns of species abundance, and the shape of a patch may determine which species can use it as habitat. The interaction between the processes of a species' dispersal and the pattern of a seascape determines the temporal dynamics of the species' populations. Populations of wide-ranging organisms may not be as strongly affected by the spatial arrangement of habitat patches as more sedentary species are, which brings me to "marine protected areas."

## Do No Harm

Marine protected areas are spatially defined marine units in which one or more human activities—particularly fishing—are restricted or prohibited. They represent an ecosystem-based approach to using the oceans for our human benefit based on the *precautionary principle: "Do no harm."* As such, marine protected areas are best seen as tools that complement other approaches aimed at the sustainability of marine resources. Unlike terrestrial parks and nature reserves, marine protected areas can disrupt livelihoods, especially if a protected area provides few tangible benefits to local people who have traditionally depended on it. On the other hand, they attract scientists, tourists, as well as others interests, thereby creating a complex system for protection. Fortunately, however, more effort is being devoted to enhancing habitat connectivity by creating networks of marine protected areas. Nevertheless, one widespread threat to the sustainability of these areas is climate change, which may require further increases in their size—or significant shifts in where they are located.

There will undoubtedly be resistance to the establishment of a network of marine protected areas as the *central component of a sustainable, ecosystem-based fishery.* Such resistance will manifest in large measure because of the newness, novelty [sic], and inherent constraints of the approach, whereas species-specific fisheries management has a long, *economically defined* history. Moreover, decisions about the size of protected areas, their site selection, and the disturbance levels within them may be difficult due to the relative variability and complexity of marine ecosystems.

Our responsibility now is to make our best biophysically decisions about patterns across the seascape, while considering the consequences of those decisions on the ocean's potential productive capacity for generations to come. Although the decisions are up to us, one thing is crystal clear. The current trend toward overfishing and the subsequent fragmentation of various areas of the seascape may help maximize short-term monetary profits and current lifestyles, but it devastates the long-term biophysical sustainability and adaptability of the oceans and thus plays a role in devastating their potential capacity for long-term productivity.

## Bold New Measures Save Tuna

To counter some of this degradation, representatives of Western Pacific island nations put the finishing touches on a series of bold, new measures during the last week of May 2009, decisions aimed at saving the world's last great stocks of tuna. They decided to bar fishing in two huge pockets of international waters, creating the largest ever no-fishing zone. The result is four no-take areas totaling 745,645 square miles stretching from French Polynesia to Palau—a distance of 4,350 miles. When combined, the no-take zones are more than three times the size of California and dwarf the 223,695 square-mile protected area in the Northwestern Hawaiian Islands, whose waters contain far fewer fish. Fishing in the rest of the Western Pacific is regulated by the Western and Central Pacific Fisheries Commission, a treaty-based organization that includes 15 island nations and 10 countries that pay for the right to fish in their so-called Exclusive Economic Zones, which stretch 200 nautical miles from land.

## Interconnected Marine Protected Areas

However, it is not the relationship of numbers that confers sustainability on ecosystems. Sustainability flows from the patterns of relationship that have evolved among the various species. A relatively stable, culturally oriented seascape, even a very diverse one, which fails to support these ecologically co-evolved relationships, has little chance of being sustainable.

To create viable, culturally oriented seascapes, we must begin now to work toward the connectivity of habitats because biophysical sustainability—thus adaptability—depends on such connectivity. We must therefore ground our culturally designed protected areas within Nature's evolved patterns and take advantage of them if we are to have a chance of creating a good-quality marine environment that is ecologically adaptable.

If we are to have adaptable seascapes with sustainable productive capacities to pass to our heirs, we must focus on four primary things: (1) caring for and protecting/creating the sustainable connectivity and biological richness among the different components of the seascape, (2) specifically locating protected areas in the most heavily fished locations, (3) protecting existing biodiversity—including habitats—at any price for the long-term sustainability of the biophysical wholeness and the species richness of the patterns we create across global seascapes, and (4) the *personal willingness to change our thinking* from the narrow confines of our old, institutionalized, self-centered point of view with its endless attempts at symptomatic, quick fixes to embrace a systemic view for the social-environmental sustainability and long-term productivity of the world's oceans for *all* generations.

> "The [marine protected area] process was overseen not only by an oil industry lobbyist, but by a marina developer, coastal real estate executive and other corporate operatives."

# Marine Protected Areas Unfairly Hamper Fishing Interests and Offer Limited Environmental Benefits

*Dan Bacher*

*Dan Bacher is a blogger and fishing advocate. In the following viewpoint, he argues that the marine protected areas (MPAs) established along the coast of Southern California in January 2012 are not in the best interest of coastal communities. He claims that the MPAs ban fishing yet do not ban more-devastating activities, such as oil drilling or aquaculture, thus showing an unfair bias toward corporate interests. Bacher cites several members of Southern California coastal communities who feel that the MPAs are a danger to their livelihoods.*

As you read, consider the following questions:

1. How many square miles of state waters does the author claim will be covered by the MPA in Southern California discussed in the viewpoint?

2. According to the author, who has funded the initiative that created the MPAs?

3. According to Bacher, what is the basis for the appeal against Judge Ronald Prager's decision?

So-called marine protected areas (MPAs), created under the leadership of a big oil lobbyist, went into effect today, January 1, [2012,] in Southern California ocean waters from Point Conception in Santa Barbara County to the U.S./Mexico border.

Representatives of the Department of Fish and Game, corporate "environmental" NGOs [nongovernmental organizations], the Western States Petroleum Association, Safeway Stores and other supporters of the privately funded Marine Life Protection Act (MLPA) Initiative have reason to celebrate the beginning of the New Year with the implementation of these questionable "marine protected areas."

Walmart Chairman Rob Walton, who has dumped millions into groups supporting the MLPA Initiative and similar efforts to privatize the oceans worldwide, is no doubt very pleased also with the implementation of this network of 50 MPAs.

## The Makeup of the MPAs

This network includes 13 pre-existing MPAs retained at the northern Channel Islands and two special closures covering approximately 354 square miles of state waters and representing approximately 15 percent of the region.

In contrast, fishermen, grassroots conservationists, environmental justice advocates, civil liberties activists and those who care about openness and transparency in government oppose the privatization of the public trust view January 1, 2012 as a dark day in California history. Unlike representatives of Wall Street–funded NGOs, respected environmental leaders including John and Barbara Stephens-Lewallen fiercely oppose the privatized MLPA Initiative overseen by ocean industrialists and corporate operatives.

There are five points that are key to understanding the truth about the alleged "marine protected areas" that went into effect in Southern California waters today.

## Controlled by Corporate Interests

First, these "marine reserves" were created by the MLPA "Blue Ribbon Task Force" for the South Coast chaired by Catherine Reheis-Boyd, the president of the Western States Petroleum Association. Reheis-Boyd is a big oil industry lobbyist with an egregious conflict of interest in the designation of MPAs, considering that she has repeatedly called for new oil drilling off the California coast and the weakening of environmental regulations, as well as supporting environmentally destructive Canadian tar sands drilling. She was the proverbial "fox" in charge of the "hen house."

Second, the MLPA process was overseen not only by an oil industry lobbyist, but by a marina developer, coastal real estate executive and other corporate operatives and political hacks with numerous conflicts of interest.

Third, in a parody of true marine protection, these fake "marine protected areas" fail to protect the ocean from oil spills and drilling, pollution, military testing, corporate aquaculture, wind and wave energy projects and all human impacts on the ocean other than fishing and gathering.

Fourth, the MLPA Initiative that created the MPAs is privately funded by the shadowy Resources Legacy Fund Foundation, setting a bad precedent for the privatization of conservation and the public trust in California.

## Anglers Oppose Marine Protected Areas

Bernie Bjork ... sees the creation of a marine reserve as one more nail in the coffin of Oregon's commercial fishing fleet. "Since 1999, 80 percent of the trawl fleet's fishing grounds off the coast of Oregon and Washington have been closed down," he told me. He's not an unreasonable guy. A few years ago he worked with Environmental Defense to help establish quota systems on the West Coast. But the politics of the whole process frustrated him. "They said they'd allow boats to come in, but you can't fish. And then they said the crabbers could come in, but not the trawlers. They're going to use 'adaptive management,' which means they can change the rules at any time."

*Bruce Barcott, Environment 360, June 16, 2011. http://e360.yale.edu.*

## "Marine Poaching Areas"

Five, the California Fish and Game Wardens Association has opposed the creation of new marine protected areas until sufficient funding to patrol the existing ones is found. This is why rank-and-file game wardens refer to the MPAs as "Marine Poaching Areas."

Jeff Krieger, avid Southern California kayak angler and conservationist, sadly noted two weeks before today's closure, "I'm going to kayak fish and visit the Point Dume area this weekend and say goodbye, since this area closes on January 1. This not a victory for the 99%! It is more like a water grab by the 1%, in my mind!"

"People need access to sustainable ocean food for nutritional health and our livelihood," commented John Stephens-

Lewallen, the North Coast environmental leader who co-founded the Ocean Protection Coalition and North Coast Seaweed Rebellion and has been a vocal critic of the MLPA process. "We can't let these areas, closed by a corrupt private process, keep us from exercising our fundamental rights and duties to have access to sustainable food from the ocean."

## The Privatization of the Oceans

"The MLPA is the beginning of the privatization of our natural resources in California where, in an underhanded and illegal way, the decisions have been taken from the people and put into the hands of the ocean industrialists," said Barbara Stephens-Lewallen, John's wife and co-owner of Mendocino Sea Vegetable Company.

Those who believe in environmental justice, democracy and true, wholistic marine protection—as opposed to privately funded green washing—are committed to fighting the MLPA Initiative through litigation and exposing the numerous conflicts of interest and violations of state and federal laws.

## Hope for Overturning the Regulations

A recent appeal of an unfavorable court ruling gives California's fishing and boating community renewed hope for overturning regulations imposed under the privately funded Marine Life Protection Act (MLPA) Initiative. Coastside Fishing Club, one of the three petitioners in litigation before the San Diego Superior Court challenging MLPA regulations adopted by the California Fish and Game Commission for the North Central Coast, filed an appeal with California's 4th District Court of Appeal on December 15 [2011].

Coastside's appeal arises from the denial by Judge Ronald Prager on October 17, 2011 of its request for a Writ of Mandate [a court order to a government agency or another court to follow the law and correct prior action] voiding MLPA regulations adopted by the commission for California's North Central Coast in 2009 based on legal defects in implementing California law. After a careful review, Coastside concluded that Judge Prager's ruling is inconsistent with the mandates of the law as established by the legislature.

"It's in the best interests of all Californians that our state's laws be implemented in a fair and even-handed manner as the legislature directs," said Rick Ross, Coastside's president. "Coastside intends to pursue this legitimate goal through all available legal means. We strongly believe in the merits of our case, and the appeal process provides a fresh opportunity to have our claims considered in a different forum."

The outcome of the appeal of Judge Prager's ruling on the North Central Coast regulations would likely influence the resolution of a similar challenge to the validity of the South Coast regulations brought in the same lawsuit by Coastside's co-plaintiffs, United Anglers of Southern California and Robert C. Fletcher.

| *"The Clean Water Act [is] a vehicle to address the deleterious impact of ocean acidification."*

# The Clean Water Act Can Help Fight Ocean Acidification

*Kate Halloran*

*Kate Halloran is a doctoral candidate at American University's Washington College of Law. In the following viewpoint, Halloran cites the Center for Biological Diversity, which argues that the national Clean Water Act can be a tool in the fight against ocean acidification once there are better criteria for water quality. Halloran discusses the roadblocks to implementing clean water criteria across the nation. The Clean Water Act, she argues, has to provide a roadmap regarding what constitutes clean water, as well as the acceptable limits of pollutants. In order for it to be effective in fighting ocean acidification, Halloran concludes, the Clean Water Act has to facilitate cooperation across state borders and provide regulations for carbon emissions from a variety of sources. (Note: References in original article have been deleted.)*

As you read, consider the following questions:

1. According to Halloran, what needs to be revised first before the Clean Water Act can be used to counteract ocean acidification?

2. According to Halloran, how does the geography of the ocean challenge the Clean Water Act?

3. Why, in the author's opinion, are airborne pollutants a challenge to the Clean Water Act?

National legislation addressing the effects of climate change on our ecosystem has failed to materialize, but environmental advocates have sought other avenues to jumpstart the process. The Center for Biological Diversity, for example, has advanced the Clean Water Act as a vehicle to address the deleterious [harmful] impact of ocean acidification on marine organisms. Ocean acidification, which some scientists argue has been caused by anthropogenic [human-made] climate change, alters the chemistry of ocean water and threatens marine biodiversity. As oceans absorb carbon dioxide, pH levels decrease. The decreased pH levels inhibit the ability of many marine organisms, such as coral and plankton, to form protective shells integral to their survival. Loss of these organisms would echo throughout the marine ecosystem. The integrity of the ocean ecosystem is significant not only from an environmental standpoint but also from an economic perspective. If marine biodiversity suffers irreversible damage from ocean acidification, the effects would ripple throughout the commercial realm, impacting the fishing and tourism industries.

In 2007, the Center for Biological Diversity filed a petition with the United States Environmental Protection Agency ("EPA") requesting an update to existing water quality criteria under section 304(a) of the Clean Water Act ("CWA"). The Center for Biological Diversity argued that the pH water quality criteria required revision in light of new scientific data on the impacts of ocean acidification. EPA agreed to evaluate these concerns and published a notice in the Federal Register requesting scientific data on the issue. Despite this agreement, EPA approved a list of impaired waters in Washington that ignored ocean acidification's impacts on the state's coastal waters. The Center for Biological Diversity responded with a lawsuit against EPA. Now, as part of a legal settlement, EPA has issued a notice in the Federal Register soliciting comments on how to address ocean acidification through listing of impaired waters under section 303(d) of the CWA.

## Implementing Water Quality Criteria

The efforts of the Center for Biological Diversity are an important step forward, but the question remains how effective the CWA would be in protecting marine biodiversity from ocean acidification. Section 403(a)(2)(B) of the CWA requires that water quality criteria address "the factors necessary for the protection and propagation of shellfish, fish, and wildlife . . ." Once section 304(a) water quality criteria are determined, those criteria must be enforced. Section 303(d) is primarily a mechanism for implementing water quality criteria: first, a state compiles a list of waters within its jurisdiction that fail to meet the criteria; and second, the state establishes limits for discharges of pollutants affecting each impaired water body through Total Maximum Daily Loads ("TMDLs"). TMDLs generally are effective for managing point sources, where discharge of a particular pollutant is easily traceable and quantifiable. TMDLs for non-point sources present an obstacle for ensuring compliance and enforcement, an especially important consideration when limiting carbon dioxide emissions in ocean waters.

One challenge is determining if and how much non-point sources of carbon dioxide emissions are impacting a coastal area. If that impact can be quantified, there is still the difficulty of attributing those emissions in a way that would promote successful compliance with TMDLs. Currently, TMDLs for non-point sources "are implemented through a wide variety of State, local, and Federal programs, which are primarily voluntary or incentive-based."

## An Integrated System Is Needed

Moreover, the geography of the ocean calls for an integrated system of managing ocean acidification. Coastal waters are shared among different states that may have varying water quality criteria, impaired waters lists, and TMDLs. A state only has jurisdiction over its territorial waters, but the reality of managing a vast ecosystem requires cooperation among coastal states to prompt meaningful change.

Another potential issue is regulating carbon dioxide emissions from point sources. Discharges from point sources would require a permit through the National Pollution Discharge Elimination System ("NPDES"). Regulating carbon dioxide discharges into oceans may necessitate developing new NPDES permits that incorporate adjusted water quality criteria for ocean acidification to set effluent limitations for discharges, which could be a lengthy and complex process.

## A Time-Sensitive Issue

A final obstacle is the CWA's capacity to regulate airborne carbon dioxide emissions. Airborne carbon dioxide emissions contribute to the problem, but are not a conventional source of water pollution. While it may be possible to regulate airborne emissions under the CWA, the efficacy of doing so is questionable.

There is no doubt that ocean acidification is a time-sensitive issue endangering the health of our oceans and marine life. The prospect of using the CWA to counteract ocean acidification has focused attention on this often overlooked problem, but is not without its drawbacks. The challenges of implementing these changes serve as a reminder that ocean acidification must be attacked from more than one angle in order to maximize the chance of success in protecting marine biodiversity.

> *"[An] ocean health ... index rolls into one number the condition of the many potential benefits we receive from the ocean [and] has strategic value for policymakers, managers, and the public."*

# Three Reasons for Creating a Single Ocean Health Index

*Ben Halpern, Karen McLeod, and Jameal Samhouri*

*Ben Halpern is the director of the Center of Marine Assessment and Planning at the University of California at Santa Barbara. Karen McLeod is the director of science for COMPASS, a communications service for scientists at Oregon State University, and Jameal Samhouri is a marine ecologist at the Northwest Fisheries Center of the National Oceanic and Atmospheric Administration. In the following viewpoint, these authors compare the Ocean Health Index to the gross national product. They assert that combining different ideas of ocean health into a single index provides an impetus for promoting the health of all oceans and shore communities. The authors cite three reasons for this assertion: (1) the index assigns relative importance to different components of health; (2) the index addresses necessary trade-offs; and (3) the index provides a touchstone for communicating about and creating policies promoting ocean health.*

As you read, consider the following questions:

1. According to Halpern, McLeod, and Samhouri, who was Simon Kuznets?

2. According to the authors, how many goals will the Ocean Health Index track?

3. What in the authors' opinion is the downside of the Ocean Health Index?

Just over 75 years ago, there was no easy way to track how well a nation's economy and its people were doing. Data from all kinds of measures existed, but it was hard to interpret what they all meant. Responding in part to the dramatic declines of the Great Depression, the U.S. Congress in 1934 asked renowned economist Simon Kuznets to develop a method for gauging the condition, or health, of the United States. He came up with what we now know as the gross domestic product, or GDP.

Although criticisms abound about its utility or appropriateness as a measure of national well-being (including from Kuznets himself), the use of GDP has had an indelible and transformative impact on global economics, policy, and markets.

But why is a single index necessary or useful? Instead, why not track how the individual components are doing? Perhaps the value has become evident in the case of GDP, but it's worth diving deeper into that question since it's the philosophical foundation for why we are creating an Ocean Health Index.

There are three reasons why it is essential to synthesize information into a single index:

# 1. It forces us to make explicit the relative importance of the different components that we are evaluating.

Why not just make them all equally important? No one actually does this. People inevitably value particular attributes over others, they just do it in their heads. Whether it's the national economy, choosing a vacation destination, or what to do on a Saturday afternoon, you assess the relative importance of all the variables you value before you make a final decision. When you take a date to a restaurant, you consider price, decor, type of food, noise level, how romantic the place is, and so on, and then decide based on which variable (or variables) is most important to you. In these cases, you are weighting the importance of different criteria and making a single decision.

Market researchers spend enormous amounts of money trying to understand what qualities are most important to people. In other words, they are trying to make explicit and quantitative the weights that people place on different decision criteria.

Those of us creating the Ocean Health Index are doing exactly the same thing. By combining the very different goals people have for a healthy ocean into a single number, we force ourselves to make explicit how important each of those goals is to defining a healthy system; we crystallize the weights we place on the different components. Some people will care most about jobs and livelihoods, for example, while others will care more about biodiversity conservation and clean water. There is no right or wrong answer. We all have legitimately different views of what we want from a healthy ocean. However, we need to find ways to reconcile these conflicting views, as decisions about ocean use (and non-use) affect the well-being of all people, now and in the future.

This may seem a difficult challenge, but any environmental management decision faces this same issue. We plan to generate weightings for different goals in the OHI in at least three ways. Our hope is to understand how perceptions of

## The Benefits of the Ocean Health Index

[The Index] recognizes that people are now part of the ocean ecosystem and defines a healthy ocean as one that sustainably delivers a range of benefits to people now and in the future. Doing so requires a much more thoughtful and forward-looking partnership between people and oceans than we have achieved to date. But it's difficult to manage what you cannot measure, which is why accounting for and valuing natural capital from our oceans is so critical.

Given all that we now know, it is absolutely essential for us to choose a smarter path; one which collectively embraces more intelligent, effective management of our natural resources. The Ocean Health Index will measure our progress along this new path and also give insight into ways to improve its score.

*Greg Stone,* Huffington Post, *June 21, 2012.*
*www.huffingtonpost.com.*

ocean health might change when viewed through different lenses: assuming equal weights for different goals (probably not right for anyone, but at least it's egalitarian), creating weightings for the goals based on different hypothetical value sets (conservationist vs. resource extraction vs. sustainable user), and surveying people representing a diversity of interests related to the ocean along the U.S. West Coast.

## 2. It makes explicit and quantitative the trade-offs that occur among goals.

Although we divide and track each of the 10 public goals of ocean health separately, they are all connected by the bio-physical world and human communities that underlie them.

This vast network of connections and the limitations it necessarily imposes mean that the output of some goals go down when others go up. Every single decision related to ocean health—whether to limit or encourage coastal development, for example—has multiple consequences, some considered good and others bad depending on who is viewing them. Such trade-offs are ubiquitous in management and policy-making—if every situation were a win-win, politicians would be out of a job. By combining the goals into a single index, these trade-offs become quantitative and obvious, and far more informative for management decisions.

Take a situation where the provision of food from fisheries and aquaculture increases by 10 percent but this comes with a 10 percent decrease in biodiversity (a certain number of species or habitats are lost from the area). For those in need of a daily meal, this change will be seen as a welcome improvement; for those who cannot bear the loss of even a single species, that outcome would be disastrous. These issues, the bread and butter of economics and public policy, require boiling everything down to a single number to be able to fairly and quantitatively assess these trade-offs. Doing so gives perspective on how disparate changes influence the big picture.

## 3. It's a much-needed communication device.

GDP has transformed the way we think about the health of a nation (and has inspired numerous alternate measures, such as [the South Asian nation of] Bhutan's Gross Domestic Happiness Index). Regardless of the exact formulation, there is tremendous utility in being able to communicate about the overall state of the nation, a concept that resonates with a broad, diverse set of audiences and potential users.

The Ocean Health Index has been developed with a similar endpoint in mind. Ocean health is an enormously complex topic; the index rolls into one number the condition of the many potential benefits we receive from the ocean. This singularity has strategic value for policymakers, managers, and the public in and of itself.

Are there downsides to generating a single number? Rolling lots of information into a single number masks a lot of detail. If people *only* pay attention to the single index score, then a lot of valuable information is lost about why a particular place received a particular score or what might be done to improve it. By our design, then, one can look under the hood of the single value to see the rich array of information regarding the ability of the ocean to deliver individual public goals. This more detailed information is available for those more interested in specific benefits or trade-offs among particular subsets of goals.

It's hard to know if Kuznets would be happy with how his GDP measure altered the global landscape, but since he saw its power in his lifetime, it's unlikely he would be surprised that it did. Economic and policy decisions require an understanding of both the big picture and the nature of the interactions and trade-offs among the component parts of that big picture. Ultimately, we hope that the Ocean Health Index can have a similar impact on decision-making and public understanding of how we interact with and benefit from the ocean.

# Periodical and Internet Sources Bibliography

*The following articles have been selected to supplement the diverse views presented in this chapter.*

Alyssa Carducci      "Alaska Officials Speak Out Against New National Ocean Policy," Heartland Institute, June 4, 2012. http://heartland.org.

Jo Confino      "Rio+20: Greenpeace Declares War on the Finance Sector," *The Guardian* (Manchester, UK), June 19, 2012.

Doc Hastings      "Obama's National Ocean Policy Threatens Jobs and Economic Activities Onshore and Off," Fox News, June 19, 2012. www.foxnews.com.

Nicola Jones      "Ocean Health Index Devised," *Nature*, February 20, 2012.

Jane J. Lee      "US National Ocean Policy: No Success Without Science?," *Science*, May 7, 2012.

Matthew J. Oldach      "Marine Protected Areas Not Effective Against Climate Change," *Matthew Oldach* (blog), June 20, 2012. www.matthewoldach.scienceblog.com.

Cassandra Profita      "Is the Clean Water Act Really Keeping Northwest Waterways Clean?," Oregon Public Broadcasting *Ecotrope* (blog), June 8, 2012. www.opb.org/news/blog/ecotrope.

Sofia Tsenikli      "Rio+20 Not the Oceans Summit but High Seas Protection Gains Support and Prominence," Greenpeace, June 29, 2012. www.greenpeace.org.

CHAPTER 3

# What Strategies Would Best Promote Sustainable Fishing?

# Chapter Preface

In April 2012 the supermarket chain Whole Foods decided to stop selling seafood that is not considered sustainable. This ban has stirred controversy over the very idea of sustainable fishing.

New England fisheries are hit particularly hard by the outright ban on harvesting gray sole and skate, which are common catches in the region, and a ban on keeping cod that has been caught by bottom trawling, a common fishing method in the area. Even though Whole Foods is but one chain, commercial fishers are worried about the message such a ban may send. "Whole Foods is a reputable, credible food source for a big community of people, and so when their headquarters makes this kind of statement, it's not good for the industry," writes Abby Goodnough in an April 21, 2012, *New York Times* article, and may potentially cause other chains to follow suit, which could seriously hamper the economy of the region. Members of the New England fishing industry are outraged by what they perceive to be a misguided marketing ploy meant to please the typically "green" customer base of Whole Foods. "We have the strictest management regime in the world, . . . so using the word 'sustainable,' maybe it looks good in your advertising, but, without being too harsh, it means absolutely nothing," argues David Goethel, a member of the New England Fishery Management Council quoted by Goodnough.

Whole Foods claims that it is addressing the very real problem of overfishing, which endangers biodiversity, hoping that the ban will allow badly depleted stock to recover. "As of Earth Day 2012, we no longer carry red-rated wild-caught fish in our seafood departments! It's our way of supporting our oceans and helping to reverse overfishing trends," explains the supermarket chain's website. Whole Foods follows the guidelines of its partners, the Marine Stewardship Council and the

Blue Ocean Institute, yet the selective ban has raised some questions regarding what exactly is—or is not—labeled "sustainable." "Some fishermen questioned why Whole Foods would approve net-caught fish, as marine mammals are known to get entangled in gillnets, and hook-caught fish, as hooks often end up catching undersize fish," adds Goodnough.

And indeed, even fisheries approved by the Marine Stewardship Council are not above reproach. A report of a study by the Heimholtz Centre for Ocean Research in Kiel, Germany, published in the journal *Marine Policy* in 2012, states:

> [Our study] examines seafood stocks that were certified by the Marine Stewardship Council (MSC) or Friend of the Sea (FOS). Stock size and fishing pressure were compared with the internationally agreed reference points, which both organizations have accepted. No suitable status information was found for 11% (MSC) to 53% (FOS) of the certified stocks. For the stocks with available status information, 19% (FOS) to 31% (MSC) had overfished stock sizes and were subject to ongoing overfishing.

Given that the concept of sustainable fishing is subject to interpretation, attempting to agree upon sustainable fishing practices in fisheries seems an futile task. The viewpoints in the following chapter debate the sustainability of fishing strategies such as maximum sustainable yield, catch share programs, and offshore fish farming.

| "[Maximum sustainable yield] will lead
| to larger [fish] stocks."

# Maximum Sustainable Yield Policies Can Save Fish Stock

*European Commission*

*The European Commission is the executive governing body of the European Union. The directorate-general for Maritime Affairs and Fisheries of the European Commission manages the European Union's integrated maritime policy and common fisheries policy. In the following viewpoint, the commission (via the the Maritime Affairs and Fisheries directorate-general) proposes that the principle of maximum sustainable yield (MSY) improves the numbers and health of the fish stock, which leads to a higher financial yield for members of the fishing industry. Using examples of fisheries across Europe, the commission shows that the principle of MSY can be introduced successfully. The commission proposes that in mixed fisheries the most vulnerable stock should decide the maximum sustainable yield to ensure the health of the entire fishery. The commission further proposes to offset financial hardships for the fishing industry by funding MSY practices.*

As you read, consider the following questions:

1. What does the commission call a vicious circle?

2. According to the author, what other measures should fishers use to reduce impact on vulnerable fish stock?

3. How, in the author's opinion, can small-scale fishers receive funding from the European Maritime and Fisheries Fund?

Seventy-five percent of EU [European Union] fish stocks are overfished, compared to 25 percent on average worldwide. This overfishing in the EU damages fish stocks, leads to uncertain catches and makes our fishing industry financially vulnerable. Fragile fish stocks lead to suboptimal catches and this in turn leads to more fishing. Today, overfished stocks are mostly made up of smaller and less-valuable fish. These are discarded back into the sea either because of their low commercial value or because they are below the minimum size.

## Maximum Sustainable Yield

We have to break this vicious circle. This is the idea behind MSY [maximum sustainable yield], which is the largest catch that can be taken from a fish stock over an indefinite period without harming it. Managing stocks according to MSY will mean going from fishing desperately on smaller fish stocks to fishing rationally on abundant ones. It will lead to larger stocks, and thus higher catch potential, higher profit margins and higher return on investment—in other words, an additional income for our fishing industry. It will also bring larger fish in the catches fetching higher market prices per kilogramme. With less undersized fish in the hauls there will be less pressure to discard. Furthermore as it takes less fishing time to catch a tonne of fish from an abundant stock than from a smaller one, this will also reduce fuel expenditures as well as carbon emissions of fishing vessels. Finally, consumers will have a much wider choice of fish from healthy EU stocks.

Member States (MS) and the EU subscribed to the MSY objective almost thirty years ago in the 1982 UN Convention on the Law of the Seas. They then reiterated it in the 1995 UN Fish Stock Agreement, in 2002 in the Johannesburg Declaration and finally in 2010 in Nagoya [Japan]. Important international partners, such as the United States and Australia, have already moved in this direction, and the EU is lagging behind.

## Long-Term Plans Are Best

The best way to manage fish stocks according to MSY is through multiannual plans. Fixing the fishing mortality to be achieved by a plan is the best management measure to ensure stability from one year to the next. The multiannual plans should fix mortality rates at a level that can help us obtain larger stocks over time.

A number of existing long-term management plans are based on the MSY principle. Since 2010 the Commission bases its proposals for annual TACs [total allowable catch] and quotas on scientific advice and on achieving MSY by 2015. The fishing industry in Europe has proven that it is possible to move to MSY, because we have already achieved it for 11 stocks, namely sole in the Skagerrak, Kattegat and Baltic Sea, in the western Channel, in the Celtic Sea; North Sea haddock, Rockall haddock; herring in the North Sea, the west of Scotland and the Celtic Sea, megrims off Spain and Portugal and North Sea Nephrops. All of these stocks are today fished sustainably with increased landings and incomes for the fishermen and the coastal communities. Furthermore for a number of other stocks we are on a good way towards MSY 2015. Eastern Baltic cod is a show case where determined action has brought the fisheries from serious overexploitation to sustainable exploitation and quotas are increasing year on year.

In order to have reliable information to determine MSY we need to have reliable data on fishing. Two developments under the reform will bring about this reliable data: firstly, the

## Regulation Cannot Just Be Catch Limits

Trying to regulate a fishery merely by setting catch limits is like controlling a land vehicle—car or locomotive—by using only its brakes. What really matters is control of the fuel flow, of the energy input. Brakes can have a secondary role—preventing disaster if an unexpected bend appears, or descending slope or obstruction ahead. If brakes are used without appropriate adjustment of the fuel flow first the wheels will overheat and eventually the vehicle is likely to be destroyed! One of the most efficient machines ever designed, a modern yacht, has no brakes, only sophisticated controls, by main-sail alignment and rudder of the input of the energy of the wind. Perhaps the better analogy to fisheries management is the control system of an aircraft—motor or, better, sailplane. Input in the landing routine is control of angle with the elevators, using adjustment to gravity to limit the approach speed. There are brakes—the airbrakes in the wings—but no pilot would dream of relying only or mainly on those to bring his craft to a safe standstill.

*Sidney Holt, Breaching the Blue, November 7, 2011.*
*http://breachingtheblue.com.*

obligation to land all catches (as opposed to the current estimates of discard data); secondly, the new partnerships between fishermen and scientists. These will improve the collection of more reliable catch data and will significantly improve the knowledge base to determine MSY.

## Stock Vulnerability Sets Limits

In mixed fisheries, it should be the most vulnerable stock that determines the limits of exploitation for all other fish taken in the same fishery. This is the only way to ensure that MSY is reached for all stocks in a fishery. For instance, reaching MSY in the sole fishery requires adjusting the fisheries for plaice [flatfish] (and for other by-catch [nontargeted species] stocks) accordingly, and may imply a fishing mortality lower than MSY for plaice. At the same time fishermen can decrease the impact of fishing on the most vulnerable species by using more selective gear. Selective gears will be part of multi-annual plans and technical measures and they can be adapted by the MS via regionalization to the specific requirements of the fishery in question.

In a number of fisheries the most vulnerable stock is at the same time the most valuable one. This is for example the case for cod in the whitefish fishery and sole in the flatfish fishery. Establishing the corresponding fishing opportunities in such mixed fisheries will require fixing MSY rates for each of the stocks, and ICES [International Council for the Exploration of the Sea] is currently working on this.

In the international context the EU needs to apply the same principle as for itself. When acting on behalf of the EU, the Commission will seek to integrate the MSY objective in its negotiating position, basing itself on scientific advice or input.

## Ensuring Sustainability

There is consensus that in the medium term MSY will ensure environmental, social and economic sustainability. The issue is how to get there and the Commission is determined to help the fishing industry and the coastal communities cope with the transition. It has therefore proposed a strong EMFF [European Maritime and Fisheries Fund] with a whole catalogue of funding possibilities for the fishing industry, including funding

- for the fishing industry to develop more selective fishing methods

- for vessel owners and fishermen to participate in selectivity trials

- for social dialogue meetings of the fishing industry in and across MS to exchange ideas and best practices

- for training and professional qualifications to become familiar with innovative gears

- for diversification of small-scale fishermen

- for the fishing industry to collect specific data, be it biological or socio-economic data

- for marketing initiatives to develop product brands, such as "MSY fish"

- for fishermen to participate actively in regionalization by coming forward with concrete proposals on how to achieve MSY 2015.

> "[A maximum sustainable yield policy] requires good management, monitoring, and enforcement systems. In much of the world, these conditions simply don't exist."

# Maximum Sustainable Yield Policies Are Problematic

*Carl Safina*

*Carl Safina is an adjunct professor at State University of New York at Stony Brook's School of Marine and Atmospheric Sciences. In the following viewpoint, Safina lists reasons why the concept of maximum sustainable yield is problematic. The assumption that there is a surplus in the sea is false, he claims: Fish that do not reach adulthood are part of another species' food chain, and a surplus of eggs in one year accounts for a lack of eggs in the next. The concept of maximum sustainable yield is only useful if it is strictly enforced, Safina concludes, and that would require an unrealistic cooperation of agencies across international borders.*

As you read, consider the following questions:

1. According to the author, what are the three most typical reactions to the concept of maximum sustainable yield?

2. According to Safina, when do most fisheries consider a population overfished?

3. In the author's opinion, how can marine protected areas help create sustainable fisheries?

The idea that fisheries have a "maximum sustainable yield" [MSY] was first articulated in the mid-20th Century. . . .

Opinions on the formalized concept of "maximum sustainable yield" in fisheries seem to fall into several camps: 1) those believing the concept is sound, 2) those believing the concept is fundamentally flawed, 3) those believing it could work but has seldom really been implemented.

## No Surplus Exists in the Sea

The concept of maximum sustainable yield has obvious weaknesses. One, the basis is that the ocean (like the rest of living nature) creates "surplus production," meaning more juveniles than could possibly survive to adulthood. (Early proponents of MSY in the 1940s thought fish left in the ocean were "wasted" because they "just die.") But there really is no surplus; what fisheries scientists call "excess production," the rest of the ocean considers "food."

That leads to problem two: the thinking on MSY wholly ignores food webs. If herring, say, can realistically produce a maximum sustainable catch for humans according to MSY calculations, where does that leave things that eat herring, such as tunas, whose own MSY can't be realized if we've already eaten much of their food. Even though [this reality is] so basic, MSY doesn't account for this.

Three, MSY is focused on taking the maximum. Focusing more on the word "maximum" than on "sustainable" has proven a risky strategy because it leaves no margin of error.

## More Eggs Are Needed

Four, because fisheries scientists have assumed that there's only enough "room" in the sea for a limited number of eggs to survive to adulthood, they've been comfortable with the idea that a limited number of eggs is just fine. Most fisheries scientists don't consider a population "overfished" until it's only about one-third what it was before fishing. In other words, they consider fishing down a population until it's two-thirds depleted to be their "target," since they believe that fishing increases the productivity of the fish. Consequently, they consider a deeply depleted population to be "fully recovered" when it's really only one-third as abundant as it would be without fishing.

And they don't value very large, old fish in the ocean, because they think it's best if a fish is caught after it finishes its period of rapid growth in the prime of its life. Fish scientists, on the other hand (whose profession is the actual biology of fish, as opposed to *fisheries* scientists, whose profession is more about fishing), have in the last couple of decades shown that the biggest, oldest fish lay vastly more eggs and so are vastly more valuable as breeders. They also lay eggs that are larger, better supplied with nutrients, and therefore better poised for survival.

And finally for now, marine ecologists have shown that it's important for a population to be able to produce vastly more eggs than can survive in most years, because population abundance tends to be maintained by high survival in unusually favorable years. Since unusually favorable years are unpredictable and widely scattered, the population must be poised to take advantage of them when they occur. But that's less possible if the population is depleted and dominated by younger breeders.

## The Practical Problems

Then there are practical problems: Once you allow a population to be depleted by two-thirds because that's your "target," what do you tell the boats that were doing all that fishing? This is one of the main reasons this system hasn't worked po-

## A Fuzzy Principle

Maximum Sustainable Yield (MSY) is the largest annual catch of a particular species that fishermen can take continuously without overfishing it. The problem with MSY as an indicator of the health of the fishery is that we never know what MSY is until we have overfished the stock. Then it is an uphill battle to get back to where we were before the stock was overfished.

*Bob Enderson, William Aila, and Linda Paul,*
*Pacific Fisheries Coalition. www.pacfish.org.*

litically. On the scientific side, how should we account for natural fluctuations in population numbers, since fluctuations mean that the MSY would have to vary? Doesn't that imply that there is not really one *sustainable* yield? What is the MSY where different breeding populations—some very abundant, and some small—mix on the fishing grounds? In that case, how do we protect the weak stocks? (There are plenty of cases like that.) And what if the fishery catches different species in the same net? And what if some of those species are slow-growing and others fast? Can MSY-based management really cope with those common situations? Further, doing the calculations requires a lot of good data and good information about the fishing fleets. And applying the MSY-based numbers as real-world catch limits requires good management, monitoring, and enforcement systems. In much of the world, these conditions simply don't exist.

Even where the data are good enough, fishing industry pressure and the resulting lack of political will often causes fisheries managers to simply ignore scientists' advice. Then managers allow fishing far in excess of MSY, resulting in fish depletion.

Those might all add up to reasons enough to discard the concept. Yet, where it has been applied, MSY seems useful despite its flaws. That's probably because in a world of too many people and too much fishing pressure, any limits are better than no limits. Ever since the U.S. extended its territorial claims to 200 miles from the coast in 1976, Alaska's fisheries managers generally held catch limits to the MSY levels recommended by scientists. New England's managers often ignored scientists' recommendations and warnings. Alaska's fisheries remained healthy and profitable, but New Englands' crashed and burned. For some other fish populations, holding the catch to MSY-based levels is helping arrest declines and facilitate recovering trends.

Ending overfishing—by holding catches to the MSY, and allowing breeding populations to recover to levels capable of generating the maximum sustainable catch—is now mandated by U.S. federal law. I think this can help a lot. But I don't think it can solve all our problems. Or work worldwide.

## Enforcing the Rules Is Key

The effectiveness of all fisheries management depends on enforcement. This ranges from governmental systems to peer pressure. But enforceability depends on people understanding the rules, and a general willingness to comply. Most of the world lacks these conditions. Most of the world has also demonstrated an inability to form consensus, especially across national borders.

I am often asked where in the world there is now "effective fisheries management." If that means sustainable fishing, sensible rules, effective enforcement, recovery trends for depleted species, and a modicum of protection for non-target animals such as seabirds and turtles (where turtles are not targeted), my reply is: The United States, Canada, Australia, New Zealand, the Falkland Islands and South Georgia [islands in the South Atlantic]. That's about it. And even those places have problems. Europe, where effective management would require international discipline, suffers a chronic lack of such discipline in fisheries. Africa, South America, most of Asia, and the Antarctic suffer from poor frameworks, poor enforcement, corruption, and illegal fishing. Africa is a particularly tragic case; much of the overfishing that harms Africans is done by European boats whose owners pay underpriced fees in exchange for fishing access.

Nowadays, we seem to understand that the concept of maximum sustainable yield has limited usefulness. Seeking a truly sustainable future for fisheries, many scientists and conservationists are turning to creating networks of marine reserves which can conserve natural processes, let fish recover, and serve as breeding grounds and "factories" for fish that will leave the reserve and support fishing. Others are trying to develop a science and practice of "ecosystem-based management" that can succeed in maintaining everything from food webs to fisheries to evolution.

These ideas have a long way to go. But fisheries management has not generally succeeded, so new ideas are needed. Whether any idea can really work long-term without arresting human population growth is another question.

> "An innovative . . . fisheries manage-
> ment strategy called 'catch shares' can
> reverse fisheries collapse."

# Catch Share Can Help Avert Fishery Collapse

*CompassOnline*

*Compass is dedicated to bringing together the worlds of science, journalism, and public policy. The following viewpoint describes a scientific study of a fisheries management strategy known as catch shares by a team from the University of California at Santa Barbara and the University of Hawaii. Shareholders own a portion of the fishery stock, which creates the desire to care for and protect the long-term health of the fishery. The study's authors argue that this phenomenon has reduced the danger of fishery collapse by half. Using the example of the Alaskan halibut fishery, the authors show that catch share management leads to a positive change in fishing behavior that ensures the health and growth of the stock which ensures financially successful fishing. They argue further that fair distribution of catch share ownership and proper oversight are prerequisites for successful fisheries.*

As you read, consider the following questions:

1. In the opinion of the study's authors, who sets the limit of a fishery's total allowable catch?

2. According to Compass, how can catch share programs reduce bycatch?

3. According to the study's authors, why did the price of Alaskan halibut increase?

A study published in the September 19 [2008] issue of *Science* shows that an innovative yet contentious fisheries management strategy called "catch shares" can reverse fisheries collapse. Where traditional "open access" fisheries have converted to catch shares, both fishermen and the oceans have benefited.

Catch shares are common in New Zealand, Australia, Iceland, and, increasingly, the US and Canada. They guarantee each shareholder a fixed portion of a fishery's total allowable catch, which is set each year by scientists. Much like stock shares in a corporation, these shares can be bought and sold. Each share becomes more valuable when the fish population—and thus the total allowable catch—increases. With catch shares, every shareholder has a financial stake in the long-term health of the fishery.

The results of the study are striking: while nearly a third of open-access fisheries have collapsed, the number is only half that for fisheries managed under catch share systems. Furthermore, the authors show that catch shares reverse the overall downward trajectory [path] for fisheries worldwide, and that this beneficial effect strengthens over time.

"Under open access, you have a free-for-all race-to-fish, which ultimately leads to collapse," says lead author Christopher Costello, an economist at the Bren School of Environmental Science and Management at the University of California, Santa Barbara. "But when you allocate shares of the catch, then there is an incentive to protect the stock—which reduces collapse. We saw this across the globe. It's human nature."

## The First Global Evidence

The results of this study are certain to have wide-ranging implications as more fisheries in the United States, Canada, Mexico, and elsewhere consider switching to catch shares systems. It is particularly timely for the West Coast of the United States, where the groundfish fishery—which encompasses more than 80 species including sole, rockfish (snapper), hake, and sablefish (Alaskan black cod)—is likely to transition to catch shares. This paper provides the first global evidence that catch shares lead to better biological outcomes, and contributes an important scientific basis to the discussions. The Pacific Fisheries Management Council, which manages the groundfish fishery on the West Coast, will make their final decision on the week of November 2, 2008.

This new study also offers hope that fisheries can resist the widespread global collapse projected two years ago by Boris Worm of Dalhousie University, Halifax and colleagues. In fact, the current work uses the same dataset that Worm et al. based their projection on—a global database of fisheries from the Sea Around Us Project that spans the years 1950–2003. The authors of the present study—Christopher Costello and Steven Gaines of the University of California, Santa Barbara and John Lynham of the University of Hawaii—were motivated by that paper to investigate possible solutions. Their analysis of more than 11,000 fisheries suggests that we already have the tools to reverse the current global fisheries crisis.

"Previous papers, including my own, have relied on small samples from the world's fisheries. The great thing about this paper is they have made an attempt to find all the fisheries in the world that have used dedicated access and evaluate the consequences," says Ray Hilborn, a leading fisheries scientist at the University of Washington who was not involved in the study. "The field has now moved beyond listing failures in fisheries. Ecology and economics do not need to collide; win-win solutions have been found."

While the current study focuses on Individual Transferable Quotas (ITQs), which are a type of catch share, Costello and his co-authors note that to maximize benefits, catch shares must be tailored to the ecological, economic, and social characteristics of a fishery.

## Catch Share Reduces Bycatch

If designed properly, catch share programs can reduce by-catch—the unintentional harvest of threatened or undesirable species—and protect the ecosystem in the process. By imposing individual limits on bycatch, as well as on desirable species, catch shares create incentives to develop environmentally beneficial new technologies, such as more selective, less damaging fishing gear.

"The difference is comparable to renting an apartment versus the house you own," says Costello. "If you own something, you take care of it—you protect your investment or else it loses value. But there's no incentive for stewardship when you don't own the rights to it."

The Alaskan halibut fishery is a prime example of success. In 1995, when the fishery converted to ITQs, the total season had dwindled from about four months down to just two or three days. These dangerous sprints resulted in boats with their holds crammed full of frozen fish; by the time the over-loaded processing facilities could accommodate them, quality had suffered. Today, the season lasts nearly eight months. Because boats now haul in fresh, undamaged fish in manageable quantities, the per-pound price has increased significantly.

"Halibut fishermen were barely squeaking by—but now the fishery is insanely profitable," says co-author Steve Gaines, Director of the Marine Science Institute at the University of California, Santa Barbara.

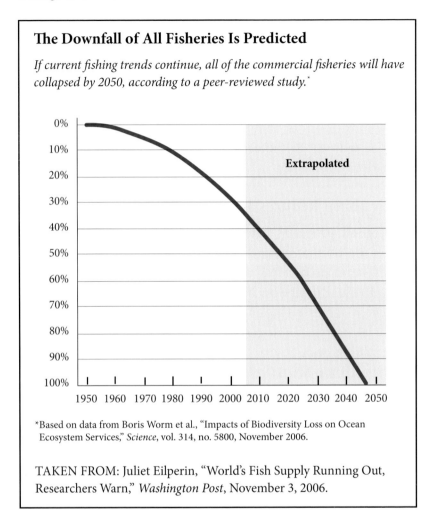

**The Downfall of All Fisheries Is Predicted**

*If current fishing trends continue, all of the commercial fisheries will have collapsed by 2050, according to a peer-reviewed study.*

Extrapolated

1950 1960 1970 1980 1990 2000 2010 2020 2030 2040 2050

*Based on data from Boris Worm et al., "Impacts of Biodiversity Loss on Ocean Ecosystem Services," *Science*, vol. 314, no. 5800, November 2006.

TAKEN FROM: Juliet Eilperin, "World's Fish Supply Running Out, Researchers Warn," *Washington Post*, November 3, 2006.

## Ownership Is Powerful

The authors emphasize that for all their strengths, catch shares are not a panacea. Strategies vary widely, and must be carefully designed and continually fine-tuned to meet the goals of the ecosystems, economies and societies they are meant to serve. Controls such as consolidation caps, which prevent any one entity from owning too much of a given fishery, and community-owned quotas have worked in some cases to help maintain vibrant ports and fisheries. Some design features however, such as how shares are allocated between individuals and processors, can be contentious, as in the Alaskan king crab fishery and elsewhere.

"One of the big challenges in catch shares is how you allocate the shares," Gaines explains. "But this is not a scientific question; it's a value judgment on the part of local communities and their governments."

Overall, the current study scientifically affirms what some fishermen and fisheries managers have long suspected based on anecdotal evidence and firsthand observation.

"Up until now, it's been an article of faith. It's pleasing to see that the data really does show these trends," says Jeremy Prince, a fisheries scientist and former fisherman from Australia who is a leader in transitioning fisheries to catch shares.

"This study gives us a solution to work with in fighting the global fishery crisis," says Boris Worm, who was not involved in the research. "There are fisheries which are doing well because of rights-based management. It's the silver lining that we have been looking for. Now we need to implement these solutions more widely."

## No One-Size-Fits-All Solution

Catch shares are not a one-size-fits-all solution. However the current study demonstrates that ownership can be a powerful ally in the effort to reverse fisheries decline, especially when deployed with complementary management strategies. With proper design, careful monitoring, and real-time adaptation to changing environmental conditions, catch shares can help ensure that the world will enjoy plentiful seafood for years to come.

"Apocalyptic assertions that fisheries management is failing . . . fail to recognize . . . the many places where management is working."

# Reports of Fishery Collapse Are Exaggerated

*Ray Hilborn*

*Ray Hilborn is a professor of aquatic sciences at University of Washington. In the following viewpoint, Hilborn argues that predictions that fish stocks will collapse by 2048 are exaggerated. Citing his own 2009 study, Hilborn claims that most ecosystems have reduced fishing to the extent that 83 percent of all fisheries should recover rather than collapse by that future date. According to Hilborn, several different management programs such as catch limits, gear restrictions, community-based comanagement, and even temporarily closing areas, were successful. He criticizes the apocalyptic visions and calls for a closer look at successful management programs to avoid future exploitation of the oceans.*

As you read, consider the following questions:

1. According to the author, for what year did Boris Worm predict the collapse of fish stock?

2. According to a study published in 2009 that Hilborn cites, how much of the fishery stock was expected to recover?

3. According to the author, does sustainable fishing change ecosystems?

If you have paid any attention to the conservation literature or science journalism over the last five years, you likely have gotten the impression that our oceans are so poorly managed that they soon will be empty of fish—unless governments order drastic curtailment [reduction] of current fishing practices, including the establishment of huge no-take zones across great swaths of the oceans.

To be fair, there are some places where such severe declines may be true. A more balanced diagnosis, however, tells a different story—one that still requires changes in some fishing practices, but that is far from alarmist. But this balanced diagnosis is being almost wholly ignored in favor of an apocalyptic rhetoric that obscures the true issues fisheries face as well as the correct cures for those problems.

## Sources of the Apocalyptic Rhetoric

To get the storyline correct, it is important to go back to the sources of the apocalyptic rhetoric. In 2006, a paper was published by Boris Worm in *Science* that received enormous press coverage. It argued that, if current trends continued, all fish stocks would collapse by 2048. Worm and his coauthors concluded their paper with the following sentence: "Our analyses suggest that business as usual would foreshadow serious threats to global food security, coastal water quality, and ecosystem stability, affecting current and future generations."

Others joined in, chief among them Daniel Pauly, who rang and continues to ring the apocalyptic note. "There are basically two alternatives for fisheries science and management: one is obviously continuing with business as usual

. . . ," wrote Pauly in 2009. "This would lead, in addition to further depletion of biodiversity, to intensification of 'fishing down marine food webs,' which ultimately involves the transformation of marine ecosystems into dead zones."

It might surprise you to learn Pauly's views are not universally held among scientists. Indeed, these papers exposed a deep divide in the marine science community over the state of fish stocks and the success of existing fisheries management approaches. Numerous critiques of the apocalyptic stance were published after the 2006 paper, suggesting that Worm et al. had greatly exaggerated the failings of "business as usual." For instance, Steve Murawski, director of scientific programs and chief science advisor, defended the U.S. fisheries management system and pointed out that the proportion of stocks overfished in the U.S. was declining, not increasing.

## Current Fishing Practices

No one disagrees on our goals for the world's fisheries stocks—we need higher fish abundances. The arguments are largely about where we are now and how we will get to higher fish abundance and lower fishing pressure. Are current fisheries management systems working to decimate [destroy] fish stocks—or rebuild them? Do we need large areas of the oceans closed to fishing to assure sustainable seafood supply? Daniel Pauly says yes to the latter question: "This transformation," he writes, "would also require extensive use of ocean zoning and spatial closures, including no-take marine protected areas (MPAs). Indeed, MPAs must be at the core of any scheme intending to put fisheries on an ecologically sustainable basis".

In an attempt to resolve this dispute, Boris Worm and I several years ago organized a set of four meetings, sponsored by the National Center for Ecological Analysis and Synthesis (NCEAS), in which we assembled a database on abundance as measured by fisheries agencies and research surveys. Participants included several of the authors of the 2006 paper as well as several people from national fisheries management agencies.

The results were published in *Science* in 2009, and showed that, while the majority of stocks were still below target levels, fishing pressure had been reduced in most ecosystems (for which we had data) to below the point that would assure long-term maximum sustainable yield of fish from those ecosystems.

About 30 percent of the stocks would currently be classified as overfished—but, generally, fishing pressure has been reduced enough that all but 17 percent of stocks would be expected to recover to above overfished thresholds if current fishing pressure continues. In the United States, there was clear evidence for the rebuilding of marine ecosystems and stock biomass. The idea that 70 percent of the world's fish stocks are overfished or collapsed and that the rate of overfishing is accelerating was shown . . . to be untrue.

The *Science* paper coming out of the NCEAS group also showed that the success in reducing fishing pressure had been achieved by a broad range of traditional fisheries management tools—including catch-and-effort limitation, gear restrictions and temporary closed areas. Marine protected areas were an insignificant factor in the success achieved.

## False Assumptions

The database generated by the NCEAS group and subsequent analysis has shown that many of the assumptions fueling the standard apocalyptic scenarios painted by the gloom-and-doom proponents are untrue:

- For instance, the widespread notion that fishermen generally sequentially deplete food webs—starting with the predators and working their way down—is simply not supported by data.

> ## Some Fish Species *Are* Overfished
>
> Jack mackerel, rich in oily protein, is manna to a hungry planet, a staple in Africa. Elsewhere, people eat it unaware; much of it is reduced to feed for aquaculture and pigs. It can take more than five kilograms, more than 11 pounds, of jack mackerel to raise a single kilogram of farmed salmon.
>
> Stocks have dropped from an estimated 30 million metric tons to less than a tenth of that in two decades. The world's largest trawlers, after depleting other oceans, now head south toward the edge of Antarctica to compete for what is left.
>
> Mort Rosenblum and Mar Cabra,
> New York Times, *January 25, 2012.*

- Declining trophic level [links in the food chain] of fishery landings is just as often a result of new fisheries developing rather than old ones collapsing.

- Catch data also show that fishing patterns are driven by economics, with trophic level a poor predictor of exploitation history.

- Furthermore, the mean trophic level of marine ecosystems is unrelated to (or even negatively correlated with) the trophic level of fishery landings.

- And the oft-cited assessment that the large fish of the oceans were collapsed by 1980 is totally inconsistent with the database we have assembled—for instance, world tuna stocks in total are at present well above the level that would produce maximum sustained yield, except bluefin tuna and some other billfish [such as marlin and swordfish] that are depleted.

Nevertheless, many in the marine conservation community appear unwilling to accept these results, continue to insist that all fish may be gone by 2048, and use declining catches in fisheries where regulations have reduced catches as indications of stock collapse.

No one argues that all fisheries are well-managed, and so far we do not have abundance estimates for many parts of the world, especially Asia and Africa. Using the catch-based methods of Worm et al. and Pauly, these areas appear to have fewer stock collapses and overfished stocks than in the areas for which we have abundance data. However, we do not know if these areas have been reducing exploitation rates or if they are still increasing.

Finally, in places without strong central government control of fishing, there is broad agreement that community-based co-management can be effective. For these fisheries, management tools are very different than those used for industrial fishery stocks, and MPAs are here often a key ingredient. The lessons from the Worm et al. paper about what works to rebuild fish stocks are applicable to industrial fisheries, but probably not to the small-scale fisheries that support many fishing communities.

## Room for Policy Debate

There is considerable room for policy debate about where we want to be in the trade-off between yield and environmental impact of fishing. There is no denying that sustainable fishing changes ecosystems, and that different societies will almost certainly make different choices about how much environmental change they will accept in return for sustainable food production. But science cannot provide the answers for this debate; it can only evaluate the trade-offs.

My perspective is that we need to treat fisheries like medical diagnoses. We must identify which fisheries are in trouble and find the cures for those individual fisheries. The evidence is strong that we can and are rebuilding stocks in many places. Let us accept that progress and identify the problem stocks and how to fix them.

Apocalyptic assertions that fisheries management is failing are counter-productive—not only because these assertions are untrue, but because they fail to recognize the long, hard work of fishery managers, scientists and stakeholders in the many places where management is working. While the gloom-and-doom advocates have been attracting public attention and press coverage, thousands of people—decried by Pauly as agents of the commercial fishing interests—have worked through years of meetings and painful catch and effort reductions to lower fishing pressure and successfully rebuild fisheries.

> *"Without thoughtful planning and regulation, fish farming can severely harm ocean ecosystems."*

# Offshore Fish Farming Poses Grave Risks to the Environment

## Ocean Conservancy

*The Ocean Conservancy is a nongovernmental organization working toward sustainability of the oceans' ecological systems. In the following viewpoint, the Ocean Conservancy argues that fish farming is not fishing, and is therefore not covered under fishing laws such as the Magnuson-Stevens Act. As it is inadequately regulated, the author claims, fish farming poses economic, legal, and environmental risks. The author maintains that the Aquaculture Fishery Management Plan proposed in 2009 aims at an increase of aquaculture within a ten-year period yet does not propose restrictions and rules that curb the risks to wild fish stock through environmental risks such as pollution of nutrients, a change in the ecosystem imparted by escaped farmed fish on the wild fish stock.*

As you read, consider the following questions:

1. According to the author, what is the currently designated area of offshore aquafarming?

2. What, according to the Ocean Conservancy, are some of the risks involved with escaped fish from fish farms?

3. When, in the author's opinion, did the Aquaculture Fishery Management Plan go into effect?

Fish farming is one of the fastest-growing responses to our declining wild fish supply and now accounts for more than 40 percent of the world's seafood consumption. Without thoughtful planning and regulation, fish farming can severely harm ocean ecosystems. Unfortunately, in the US this industry is expanding offshore for the first time without any national standards in place.

## Fish Farming Is Not Fishing

In January 2009, fishery managers in the Gulf of Mexico approved the first-ever plan for commercial-size fish farms in US federal waters, the area between three and 200 miles from shore. US fish farming—sometimes called "aquaculture"—is expected to grow five-fold by 2025, but it carries with it considerable environmental and economic risks.

The Gulf plan claimed to draw its authority from the Magnuson-Stevens Act, the nation's primary fisheries law. But there's one catch: Congress has not explicitly authorized any federal agency—not the Gulf Council, not the National Marine Fisheries Service, not anyone—to manage the farming of fish in federal waters. It is an unregulated industry, and there is no clear mandate for who should manage it.

The fact is that fish farming is *not fishing*, and therefore the nation's *fishing* laws—primarily the Magnuson-Stevens Act—are inappropriate, ineffective, and inadequate for managing this growing industry.

To ensure a safe and sustainable industry, and to protect our vast and valuable ocean, the federal government must establish strong standards for aquaculture.

## National Standards Are Needed

We need these standards now. Already, the National Marine Fisheries Service and the Gulf Council have spent over a quarter-of-a-million dollars developing their plan, but what's needed is a national vision, not a regional approach.

Here are the facts:

- Under the [George W.] Bush Administration, the National Oceanic and Atmospheric Administration set a goal to increase US aquaculture from $900 million to $5 billion annually by 2025.

- The proposed plan would grant the National Marine Fisheries Service authority to issue permits for single farms raising up to a total of 64 million pounds of fish (29 million kgs.) annually—roughly the output of 80 standard commercial fish farms today.

- Nearly all commercial wild species managed by the Gulf Council could be farmed in the Gulf of Mexico.

- The ten-year permits would be transferable. Applicants would also have to acquire a site permit from the Army Corps of Engineers and another from the Environmental Protection Agency [EPA] allowing discharge into the ocean.

- Permit applicants would have to post a bond to pay for removal of their farms in the event of trouble—but there is one key missing piece: the bond fails to cover environmental remediation.

## A Host of Environmental Risks

Open-ocean aquaculture poses a host of environmental risks, most of which are not properly addressed by the proposed management plan. Additionally, the plan's provisions for site approval do not require comprehensive scientific data that would minimize harmful impacts.

Risks from aquaculture include:

- Nutrient and chemical pollution: Feed, fish excrement, medication, and chemicals released into the ocean can affect wild fish, other species, and ocean habitats. These impacts must be fully understood and managed. The current plan relies on Clean Water Act regulations designed for land-based discharges, not discharges into the water from ocean-based fish farms.

- Escapes: The peer-reviewed scientific literature documents the harmful effects of the accidental release of farmed fish (escapes) on wild fish populations, but the plan largely ignores these risks. Impacts include reduced genetic diversity, the spread of disease, increased competition for food and habitat, increased predation, habitat alteration, and colonization. Any comprehensive plan would need to include genetic tagging or other methods of marking fish farmed in the ocean. Identification would also provide accountability in the use, and possible misuse, of ocean waters, a public resource.

- Feed: Increased demand for fish meal and fish oil needed to feed farm-raised fish may further stress sardines, menhaden, and anchovies [which are the source of these]. The Council does not currently regulate any of these fisheries, and it has not fully considered the likely impacts on them. In addition, the Council does not require any safeguards regarding the use of antibi-

otics or chemical additives in feed beyond those provided by FDA [Food and Drug Administration] and
EPA regulations.

Legal responsibility for environmental impacts is also lacking. As written, the plan requires bonds adequate to cover
only the removal of aquaculture facilities in the event of problems. Considering the likelihood of major storms and hurricanes in the Gulf of Mexico that could damage aquaculture
facilities, the impacts from escapes, habitat alteration, and
waste accumulation pose a great risk to the public. The permit
holder, not the general public, should bear the financial responsibility for any environmental damage.

## Past Criticism Goes Unheeded

In 2002, the Gulf Council began work on a Gulf-wide plan for
fish farming. This work evolved into the proposed Aquaculture Fishery Management Plan passed in January 2009. During public hearings, government agencies, conservation organizations, fishing groups, seafood business, more than 10,000
members of the public, and Congressional representatives ex-
pressly opposed the plan on legal, socio-economic, and environmental grounds. That opposition succeeded in delaying final action on the plan, but it wasn't enough. With minor
revisions, the Gulf Council narrowly approved the plan any-
way and sent it to the Secretary of Commerce for final approval.

A 60-day comment period followed. By August 2009, the
Secretary had received almost 20,000 public comments in opposition to the plan, including a joint statement from 77 national and local conservation, business, and fishing organizations. Thirty-seven members of Congress signed a letter
requesting that the Secretary decline the plan. Scientists from
across the US and Canada submitted a detailed analysis urg-
ing the Secretary to follow suit based largely on ecological
concerns.

Despite the real and scientifically-documented risks, and overwhelming public opposition, the United States now appears to be on the verge of expanding this new industry. In early September [2009], the legally dubious—and oxymoronic—"Aquaculture Fishery Management Plan" went into effect.

## Now Is the Time to Act

A number of influential bodies, including the Pew Oceans Commission, have stated that a coordinated national framework with rigorous environmental standards is a necessity before the nation's waters, including the Gulf of Mexico, are opened to aquaculture. Moving forward with the Gulf Aquaculture Fishery Management Plan sets a dangerous precedent for future piecemeal permitting decisions across the nation. Now is the time for national standards, before the industry has taken root.

In the absence of Congressional guidance, with this plan the Gulf Council and the National Oceanic and Atmospheric Administration are overstepping their authority. Congress must now take the lead and develop a precautionary national law that ensures the protection of wild fish and our ocean waters for generations to come.

> *"Environmentalists and fishermen have asserted that poorly regulated aquaculture development could degrade the environment and have negative effects on wild fish populations. Proponents of open ocean aquaculture believe it is the beginning of the 'blue revolution.'"*

# Offshore Fish Farming Offers Both Environmental Risks and Benefits

## Harold F. Upton and Eugene H. Buck

*Harold F. Upton and Eugene H. Buck are natural resources analysts for the Congressional Research Service. In the following viewpoint, they list arguments for and against offshore aquafarming. Aquafarming may interfere with wild fish stock due to nutrients, pharmaceuticals, equipment, or even species not natural to the open sea, they assert, as well as the potential threat of diseases. Supporters argue, the authors explain, that these impacts are negligible compared to the "blue revolution" aquafarming promises by counteracting overfishing while supplying food for the growing human population.*

Harold F. Upton and Eugene H. Buck, "Open Ocean Aquaculture," Congressional Research Service Report, August 9, 2010, pp. 1, 10–13. http://crs.nrseonline.org.

As you read, consider the following questions:

1. In the authors' opinion, how do proponents of offshore aquafarming explain that the use of antibiotics may not be necessary?

2. According to Upton and Buck, how does offshore aquafarming impact the price of fishmeal and fish oil?

3. In the context of aquafarming what is a nuisance animal, according to the authors?

Open ocean aquaculture is broadly defined as the rearing of marine organisms in exposed areas beyond significant coastal influence. Open ocean aquaculture operations would be located at a considerable distance from shore and subject to relatively harsh environmental conditions resulting from wind and wave action. Open ocean aquaculture employs less control over organisms and the surrounding environment than do inshore and land-based aquaculture, which are often undertaken in enclosures such as ponds.

## Offshore Aquaculture Is Controversial

Development of offshore aquaculture has become a controversial topic for aquaculturalists, environmentalists, recreational fishermen, and commercial fishermen. Many environmentalists and fishermen have asserted that poorly regulated aquaculture development could degrade the environment and have negative effects on wild fish populations. Proponents of open ocean aquaculture believe it is the beginning of the "blue revolution"—a period of broad advances in culture methods and associated increases in production. Potential outcomes are difficult to characterize because of the diverse nature of potential operations and the lack of aquaculture experience in open ocean areas. However, most agree that industry regulation is needed for orderly development of aquaculture while minimizing its effects on the environment. . . .

Proponents of open ocean aquaculture suggest that open ocean finfish aquaculture systems may produce fewer and less severe environmental impacts than those caused by nearshore aquaculture systems. This may be in part because dissolved and particulate waste products and excess feed may be assimilated and recycled more efficiently in the open ocean environment. However, the scope of any effects may vary greatly, depending on the culture technique, location, size/scale, and species raised. The present lack of knowledge—owing to limited experience, lack of research funding, and few studies focusing specifically on open ocean aquaculture—limits understanding of potential environmental concerns. Open ocean aquaculture pens would be open to the surrounding environment. Some critics of open ocean aquaculture cite concerns with the escape of fish, water pollution from uneaten feed and waste products (including drugs, chemicals, and other inputs), use of antibiotics and other animal drugs, alteration of benthic [seafloor] habitat by settling wastes, and the spread of waterborne disease from cultured to wild fish. Because of these concerns, critics of open ocean aquaculture hope that regulation of this emerging industry will be stringent.

## Aquaculture May Aid Wild Stocks

Proponents hold that open ocean waters are normally nutrient-deficient, and nutrients released from open ocean aquaculture operations may increase wild production in adjacent areas. Waste settling from large operations could alter benthic habitat. However, research indicates that, in some areas, currents keep water around fish cages well circulated, dissipating waste products quickly, resulting in minimal impact of open ocean aquaculture facilities on water quality. Critics question whether the experience with experimental facilities is relevant to future commercial operations, which will need to operate at a larger scale to be profitable. A possible solution might be to combine finfish operations with seaweed or bivalve [two-shelled mollusks such as oysters and clams] aquaculture to consume the excess nutrients. This approach is being tested by the University of New Hampshire at its open ocean aquaculture research project, but may be more appropriate for nearshore operations where waste diffusion is slower and nutrient concentrations are higher.

Another concern is whether the use of pharmaceuticals, antibiotics, growth-enhancing chemicals, other animal drugs, and antifouling agents [treatment to prevent the fouling or erosion of hulls or cages] used on gear and enclosures will adversely affect open water environments. Chemicals used in fish foods are regulated by the U.S. Food and Drug Administration, and veterinarian oversight might encourage proper application and minimize environmental impact. Drugs such as antibiotics, some of which were developed and approved for use in a contained or controlled environment, are often introduced to cultured fish in their feed. Unconsumed feed and fish waste products can pass through the containment system and be consumed by wild organisms. The use of some of these products may be declining, as efficacious vaccines eliminate the need for antibiotics and other drugs. Proponents of open ocean aquaculture suggest that, because of the more pristine and better oxygenated water conditions offshore, the use of antibiotics has not been necessary in any of the offshore areas being tested in the United States.

## The Increased Need for Fishmeal

Most fish currently proposed for open ocean aquaculture are carnivorous, and require feeds containing fishmeal and fish oil, which are obtained from wild stocks. Fishmeal and oil are produced from species such as anchovies and menhaden that are not usually used for direct human consumption. These species have a low per unit value, but large volumes can be caught and reduced (dried) to fishmeal, usually because they occur in large schools. Ecologically, forage species serve as prey for many wild carnivorous fish species such as striped bass and for sea birds.

Although the ratio is falling, generally one to two pounds of wild fish are typically required to produce one pound of farmed fish. Environmentalists question whether aquaculture production could exacerbate pressures and cause overfishing of the ocean fish stocks harvested to produce fishmeal. Others also assert it is wasteful to use fish for animal feeds instead of consuming them directly. Yet, markets for direct consumption of most species harvested in industrial fisheries do not exist. Proponents of aquaculture counter that wild fish stocks can be well managed and commercial harvest for fishmeal would occur with or without demand from open ocean aquaculture. They insist that, "Fish meal is a standard ingredient in livestock feed, and farmed fish are far more effective at converting it to edible protein than their terrestrial counterparts." In addition, a feed conversion rate of two pounds feed to one pound of farmed product is favorable compared to conversion rates for wild species. Use of a less desirable commodity to produce a more highly valued product is the basis of most livestock and aquaculture operations.

The prices of fishmeal and fish oil are likely to increase if large quantities are required for open ocean aquaculture. In 2006, the price of fishmeal nearly doubled because of lower anchovy catches in Peru and the growing demand for fishmeal from China. Concerns with price are likely to encourage researchers and aquaculturalists to improve feeding techniques to reduce waste, modify feed formulations, utilize alternatives such as waste from fish-processing plants, and experiment with herbivorous fish. Plant protein sources, such as canola, algae, or soybean meal, are being used to partially replace fishmeal, with significantly positive results emerging, especially where soybean meal is supplemented with certain essential amino acids. In some operations, the feed may contain as little as 30% fishmeal. An obstacle to increasing the amount of plant material that can be substituted for fishmeal appears to be the presence of anti-nutritional factors in the plant-derived materials. The choice of species and feeds will likely depend on profitability, and since many high-value candidate fish or shellfish species are carnivorous, the demand for fishmeal and fish oil is likely to increase in the foreseeable future.

## Aquafarming May Spread Diseases

Another concern involves the spread of fish-borne disease from aquaculture to wild populations. For example, problems with the transfer of sea lice from salmon farms to wild salmon have been reported. Disease may also spread from wild populations to farmed fish. A 2003 outbreak of infectious hematopoietic necrosis virus in British Columbia farmed salmon was confirmed to be a virus that had been circulating in wild fish for many years.

Genetic anomalies could occur if wild fish are exposed to or interbreed with hatchery-raised fish. This issue might arise if genetically modified or non-native fish escape from aquaculture facilities and interbreed with wild fish. The potential interbreeding problem can be greatly reduced if only sterile fish are farmed; fairly simple technology exists to accomplish such sterilization. Critics speculate that, since selectively bred and genetically modified fish may grow faster and larger than native fish, they could displace native fish in the short term (both through competitive displacement and interbreeding), but might not be able to survive in the wild for the long term. This is especially a concern of states (e.g., California, Maine, Maryland, and Washington) where genetically modified fish are banned within state waters but could be grown in offshore federal waters.

## Escaped Fish Could Be a Problem

A related concern is the introduction of exotic species into non-native waters, such as Atlantic salmon in British Columbia. Exotic fish may escape from open ocean facilities that may be particularly vulnerable to storms, although recent hurricanes and tropical storms in Hawaii, Puerto Rico, and the Bahamas have caused no reported damage or loss of fish in submerged cage-culture operations. The escape of Atlantic salmon has been documented in the Pacific Northwest and escapees have been recaptured in Alaskan commercial fisheries. Escapes are also common in the Atlantic where 40% of the Atlantic salmon caught in the North Atlantic are of farmed origin. The experience with salmon farming indicates that escaped fish could be a problem, either through interbreeding with closely related native species (genetic interactions) or through competitive displacement of native species. Although management techniques at net pen sites are improving and modified cage designs better prevent escapes, closed containment systems may be the only way to fully address this problem.

## Disturbing Marine Mammals

Some are concerned that offshore and underwater facilities may harm or disturb marine mammals and other wildlife. To address these concerns, current cage designs avoid the use of small diameter or loose lines or loosely hung netting to prevent the entanglement of sea turtles and marine mammals in net-pens and associated gear. Since net-pens would be under tension, the possibility that a turtle flipper or whale fluke would get tangled in lines or nets is unlikely. However, experience has shown that dolphins and other marine mammals do get entangled in fish farms. In addition, some types of shellfish farms may use ropes/longlines for settling and grow-out that could be problematic. Sound devices at farms to keep animals away could harass or harm marine mammals. Open ocean facilities could potentially affect some endangered species, such as North Atlantic right whales as they migrate, or alter essential habitat for feeding, breeding, and nursing. Also, there could be renewed interest in killing "nuisance" animals, as has been the case with salmon farmers killing seals and sea lions. There could be problems with other predatory animals, such as sharks, as well.

| *"Catch share management did not en-sure ecological sustainability [and] fish populations . . . are still overfished."*

# Catch Shares Do Not Protect Fish or the Environment

*Food and Water Watch*

*Food and Water Watch is a nongovernmental organization that aims to ensure the sustainability of water and food. In the following viewpoint the group argues that fisheries are successful not because they are based on a catch share principle but because they enforce existing catch limits. As fisheries in New Zealand and Norway show, the group contends, catch share programs alone do not discourage overfishing. Instead, the group maintains, they favor larger fishing boats with fishing gear dangerous to other marine life and encourage high-grading, the practice of discarding smaller, less profitable fish in favor of larger fish in an effort to stay within the quota. The smaller traditional fishers, the group concludes, cannot compete and end up losing their livelihoods.*

As you read, consider the following questions:

1. According to the author, where have most catch share programs been introduced?

2. According to Food and Water Watch, what is the danger of corporate-run fishing boats?

3. According to the author, what type of boats dominate catch share fisheries?

Catch shares are a system for managing our nation's fisheries that are causing consolidation in the fishing industry at the expense of the livelihoods of thousands of smaller-scale, traditional fishermen and their communities. Such programs are being heavily touted as a means to promote sustainable fishing, but a closer look reveals they do not have a positive environmental record. Catch shares can incentivize [reward] the use of larger-scale boats, more damaging gear and wasteful fishing practices that hurt fish populations and the habitats on which they depend.

## Total Allowable Catch

Catch shares divide the total amount of fish that can be caught in a year—called a total allowable catch, or TAC—into smaller portions, or quota. These are then given to fishermen and can be leased, bought and sold.

Despite the fact that TACs (which set sustainable fishing limits) are the key strategy for conserving fish populations, catch shares (which only distribute portions of that limit) are being promoted by federal government agencies as the best way to maintain fishery health. However, there are many ways to successfully implement a TAC-controlled fishery, and the National Research Council concluded that much of the political support for catch shares is "driven by faith in the assumption that privatization will foster ecological sensibility."

In fact, most catch share programs have been put into place in fisheries where TACs are already preventing overfishing (which occurs when fish populations are depleted to the point that that they can't sustain themselves). One widely cited study claiming that catch share programs can prevent wide-scale fisheries collapse failed to determine if improvements in fishery health were actually due to catch shares, rather than simply TAC enforcement. Another study shows that the results of fish conservation vary widely between fifteen North American catch share fisheries and concludes that catch share management did not ensure ecological sustainability.

Fish populations under some of the oldest catch share systems in the world are still overfished. In New Zealand, the percentage of assessed fish populations not meeting desired sustainability levels increased from 15 percent to more than 30 percent between 2006 and 2010. In another example, Norway's cod fish populations dropped to their lowest levels ever in 2006 after years of catch shares management.

## Quota Distribution

In a catch share fishery, the same total number of fish will be caught regardless of how the quota is distributed, but the transferability of catch shares allows the control of the fishery to consolidate in the hands of fewer, larger fishing operations.

Quota has traditionally been distributed to fishermen based on how much they have caught in the past. This may reward those that fish as hard and fast as possible, using gear associated with ecological damage. For example, corporate-run industrial-scale "factory fish" boats frequently use equipment that can catch large amounts of fish quickly, but can also damage the ocean floor and kill other wildlife unnecessarily in the process.

## Disincentivizing Sustainability

New research focusing on the implementation of the New England groundfish catch share program suggests that the catch shares program has replaced the traditional fishing community focus on diverse and adaptive fishing strategies that consider habitat, migratory patterns and fishing gear. So, rather

## Use It or Lose It

With common ownership there are no personal losses incurred when resources are wasted. Common ownership fosters a use it or lose it mentality. A classic example is fish in the ocean. If fishing trawlers come across a large school of fish, their incentive will be to capture as many of those fish as possible. If they don't take them someone else will. This can be contrasted, for example, with the owner of a commercial catfish pond. The incentives in this case are to cultivate the stock; take the largest fish and leave the smaller ones to grow to a more valuable size; to make sure that the fish are well fed and the water is kept clean and well oxygenated, etc. There is no concern that if you don't take the fish today someone else will. And if the resource, in this case catfish, is misused, then it is the owner that will have to bear the costs.

*Roy Cordato, John Locke Foundation, May 15, 2008.*
*www.johnlocke.org.*

than increasing fishermen's personal investment in the fishery and encouraging cooperation to spur long-term sustainable management, the program has motivated fishermen to attain short-term goals such as maximizing their quota usage and raising the value of their quota share.

## Incentives to Discard Fish

In many cases, fish populations continue to decline because the very design of most catch shares programs include incentives to discard fish. By limiting how much fish that fishermen can catch and making it too difficult to acquire additional quota, fishermen may discard smaller fish that will bring in less profit at the dock. This process, called "high-grading," can result in the death of many fish, which are tossed overboard, depleting fish populations while yielding no profit for fishermen. Similarly, "bycatch"—ocean wildlife that is unwanted or illegally caught while fishing other species—is also discarded and has prevented fisheries from recovering from overfishing.

Discarding and high-grading have been described as "an almost inevitable outcome of quota-managed fisheries," and catch shares typically increases incentives to do both, particularly in fisheries with fishermen that catch many species of fish simultaneously. Low-impact fishing with lower bycatch and reduced high-grading could be promoted through effective fisheries management, but the reverse is currently happening: larger-scale boats that are less selective in how they fish are becoming dominant in the catch share fisheries around the world.

## Catch Share Is Not the Solution

Catch share programs are not environmental protection measures. A close look at the environmental claims of proponents reveals that catch shares are not the solution to managing our ocean ecosystems sustainably. Given the devastating economic effect these programs have on coastal communities and fishermen, the United States cannot afford to pursue catch shares under the guise of environmental sustainability.

# Periodical and Internet Sources Bibliography

*The following articles have been chosen to supplement the diverse views presented in this chapter.*

| | |
|---|---|
| Erik Anderson | "Catch-Share Advocates Not to Be Trusted," Seacoastonline, November 1, 2011. www.seacoastonline.com. |
| Joe Barrios | "Maximum Sustainable Yield: A Lot of Fish in the Sea?," EcoVillageGreen, July 16, 2012. http://ecovillagegreen.com. |
| Beth Gardiner | "Finding a Sustainable Way to Farm the Seas," *New York Times*, October 27, 2010. |
| Sidney Holt | "Rescuing Sustainable Maximum Yield," Breaching the Blue, November 7, 2011. http://breachingtheblue.com. |
| Stratton Lawrence | "Catch Share Debate Divides Fishing Community," *Charleston (SC) City Paper*, April 18, 2012. |
| Claire Leschin-Hoar | "The Big Blue: Can Deepwater Fish Farming Be Sustainable?," Grist, March 23, 2012. http://grist.org. |
| Mark Schrope | "Fisheries: What's the Catch?," *Nature*, June 2, 2010. |
| Ralph Surrette | "Salmon Farming, an Industry That Needs to Be Caged," *Chronicle Herald* (Halifax, Nova Scotia), May 12, 2012. |
| Simon Taylor | "Damanaki Seeks to Cast Aside Bad Fisheries Habits," *European Voice*, July 20, 2011. |
| Craig Welch | "Plan for Huge Fish Farm in Strait Roils the Waters," *Seattle Times*, October 21, 2011. |

# CHAPTER 4

# What Impact Do Human Activities Have on Marine Mammals?

# Chapter Preface

In July 2012, a manatee was returned to the open sea after a collision with a boat in Florida's coastal waters had injured her so badly she needed to be treated in captivity for several months.

This happy ending cannot hide the fact that every year dozens of manatees are hurt, some even killed, by boats in the coastal waters of Florida.

A Florida icon, manatees are docile, slow-moving, plant-eating sea mammals also found in the warm waters off the coasts of Alabama, South Carolina, and Georgia. A study by Dr. Edmund Gerstein, director of marine mammal research at the Charles E. Schmidt College of Science at Florida Atlantic University, revealed that manatees have trouble hearing the lower-frequency sound emitted by boat engines when the boats slow down in coastal waters. "Slow speed zones make sense in clear water where the boater and the manatee can see each other and therefore actively avoid encounters. However, in turbid waters where there is no visibility, slow speeds actually exacerbate the risks of collisions by making these boats inaudible to manatees and increasing the time it takes for a boat to now travel through manatee habitats thereby increasing the risk and opportunities for collisions to occur," Gerstein explains. Hard to see for boaters due to their dark color, manatees and watercraft collide all too often, causing almost a hundred manatee deaths per year in Florida alone.

"While boat accidents are a well-known danger to the Florida manatee, a small gene pool and critical habitat changes also affect the future of this marine mammal species," reports wildlife conservationist Dawn Smith. Katie Tripp, director of science and conservation at the nonprofit Save the Manatee Club, agrees: "Their greatest challenge is from modern Floridians, whose boats, development, pollution and natural resource consumption provide them with unprecedented threats."

Manatees inhabit seagrass meadows, where they feed, congregate and mate. Not only do most boating accidents occur in these shallow waters, but coastal development along the Florida shore threatens their habitat: "Wetlands and natural landscapes are paved over for development, stormwater runoff and pollutant loads to the aquatic environment can increase, which further degrades manatee habitat and threatens seagrass meadows," Tripp explains. In March 2012 the US Fish and Wildlife Service established a manatee refuge in Citrus County, Florida, to counteract these threats to manatees.

The manatee is protected by the Endangered Species Act and the Marine Mammal Protection Act, prohibiting any behavior that results in "significant habitat modification or degradation where it actually kills or injures wildlife by significantly impairing essential behavioral patterns, including breeding, feeding, or sheltering," Tripp says.

The Save the Manatee Club argues that these laws should prohibit any interaction with wild manatees. "When manatees are given food or water, their natural behavior is changed; their feeding patterns are disrupted; and their travel and migration may also be affected. Furthermore, encouraging manatees to approach boat docks is a bad idea since watercraft are a significant contributor to manatee injury and mortality," Tripp claims.

Unfortunately, the manatee has been a major tourist attraction in Florida for decades, and tours advertising a swim with these "elephants of the sea" are a mainstay of the state's tourism industry. "Despite what the Save the Manatee Club and the Today Show says, interaction with the manatees is still allowed," states Captain Mike of Sunshine River Tours. Tour operators and many swimmers believe that if they are passive and just observe the creatures, then such tours are not dangerous to the animals and can even help raise awareness of the issue and of human behaviors that are dangerous to the animals.

As the example of the Florida manatee shows, encounters with humans are potentially dangerous to marine mammals. The viewpoints in the following chapter debate whether and which human behaviors interfere with and potentially threaten marine mammal life and what, if anything, must be done to ensure that marine mammals and humans can share the waters.

> *"Deep water sonar signals sometimes used in the search for petroleum ... can damage animals whose communication frequencies fall in the same range."*

# Deepwater Exploratory Sonar Kills Dolphins and Whales

*KiPNews*

*In the following viewpoint, KiPNews reports that seismic surveys in Louisiana waters were stopped due to their deleterious effect on bottlenose dolphins. The surveys, the author explains, are used by oil companies to find viable and safe drilling grounds, and emit a sound that affects the dolphins' communication system. The viewpoint cites the National Ocean and Atmospheric Administration's reporting of hundreds of dolphin deaths caused by oil spills along the coast of Louisiana and Texas, as well as the Organization for the Conversation of Aquatic Animals' reporting of mass deaths of dolphins caused by decompression syndrome, which is commonly related to sonic booms.*

*KiPNews ("KiP" stands for "Knowledge is Power") is a website reporting subjects generally overlooked by the mainstream media.*

As you read, consider the following questions:

1. In the author's opinion, why were seismic surveys halted until after the bottlenose dolphin calving season?

2. How, according to KiPNews, do oil companies and the government use the results of seismic surveys?

3. According to the author, what was discovered during a study on the dead dolphins?

With sick and dead dolphins turning up along Louisiana's coast, federal regulators are curbing an oil and natural gas exploration company from using seismic [related to earth frequencies and vibrations] equipment that sends out underwater pulses known to disturb marine mammals.

The Bureau of Ocean Energy Management has told Global Geophysical Services Inc. to not conduct deep-penetration seismic surveys until May, when the bottlenose dolphin calving season ends. The agency says the surveys are done with air-guns that emit sounds that could disrupt mother and calf bonding and mask "important acoustic cues" [between them].

The company said it laid off about 30 workers because of the restriction, which it called unnecessary.

But environmental groups suing BOEM [Bureau of Ocean Energy Management] over the use of underwater seismic equipment say restrictions should be extended to surveyors across the Gulf of Mexico.

The new limit on exploration highlights the friction over oil drilling in the Gulf since the April 20, 2010 blowout of a BP PLC [British Petroleum Public Limited Company] well that resulted in the death of 11 workers and the largest offshore oil spill in the nation's history.

## Curbing Seismic Surveys

After the 2010 spill, the Natural Resources Defence Council [NRDC] and the Centre for Biological Diversity sued to get curbs placed on underwater seismic surveys. The environmental groups argued they harm marine mammals and that the federal government violated animal protection laws after it declared in 2004 that the surveys were safe.

The government is in settlement talks with those environmental groups, according to court documents.

"Imagine dynamite going off in your neighbourhood for days, months on end," said Michael Jasny, a senior policy analyst at the NRDC. "That's the situation these animals are facing."

Jasny said the restriction placed on Global Geophysical was a good sign, but far from enough.

In its ruling, the federal agency said it was concerned that seismic surveys could affect marine mammals, and even cause them to lose their hearing.

Amy Scholik, a fisheries biologist with NOAA [National Oceanic and Atmospheric Administration], said it was unknown what kind of effects air-guns have on bottlenose dolphins, but she said there was concern about possible effects on dolphin calves because they are vulnerable to stresses. She added that whales in Alaska have been shown to change migration routes because of seismic surveys.

George Ioup, a physics professor at the University of New Orleans studying the effects of air-guns on marine mammals, said the verdict was out on the effects of air-guns on mammals. He said BOEM seemed to be ruling "on the side of caution".

"Proving there is an effect, I don't know if that has been done," he said. "I don't think the answer is overwhelmingly simple."

## Seismic Surveys Aid Safe Drilling

The air-guns are towed at low speeds behind a survey ship and emit high-intensity, low-frequency sound waves to find

## Sonar Causes Marine Mammal Deaths

A recent study in the Proceedings of the Royal Academy said researchers had recorded deaths among marine mammals as a result of decompression sickness, primarily among beaked whales "in association with anthropogenic activities such as military sonar or seismic surveys."

*David Jolly,* New York Times, *May 28, 2012.*

geological layers. Seismic surveying is essential to drillers because they tell them where to drill and not drill.

The government also relies on the seismic data to know where it's safe to drill and to determine how much it should charge for leasing offshore blocks to oil and gas companies.

Marc Lawrence, Global Geophysical's vice president in the Gulf region, said the seismic surveys do not pose a danger to marine mammals.

"We see no hazard to them whatsoever," Lawrence said. As proof, he said dolphins routinely ride along with ships when they are conducting surveys.

He said the restriction covers an area that ranges out to about 20 miles off the Louisiana coast. He called BOEM's restriction unprecedented. His company is searching for overlooked reservoirs in areas along the central Louisiana coast: Grand Isle, Timbalier island, the West Delta and south Pelto.

This is the same area where government scientists say they have found sick and dead dolphins.

## Dolphin Deaths Are Increasing

From February 2010, NOAA has reported 180 dolphin strandings in the three parishes [counties] that surround Barataria

Bay—Jefferson, Plaquemines and Lafourche—or about 18 percent of the 1,000 estimated dolphins in the bay.

Last month [March 2012], the National Oceanic and Atmospheric Administration said it had found 32 dolphins in the bay underweight, anaemic and showing signs of liver and lung disease. Nearly half had low levels of stress hormones that help with stress response, metabolism and immune function.

Lori Schwacke, a NOAA scientist, said the dolphins' hormone problems could not definitely be tied to the oil spill but were "consistent with oil exposure".

Over the same period of time, NOAA says 714 dolphins and whales have been found stranded from the Florida Panhandle to the Texas state line, with 95 percent of those mammals found dead. Normally, the region sees 74 reported dolphin deaths a year.

Environmentalists in Peru are warning that an unprecedented number of dead dolphins are washing up on the country's shores because of the use of deep water sonar systems by the shipping industry.

It follows the discovery of 615 of the mammals in the last few weeks along a 135km stretch of coastline.

As many as 3,000 dead dolphins have been found since the beginning of Peru's summer.

## Sonar Blamed for Dolphin Deaths

Researchers at the Organisation for Research and Conservation of Aquatic Animals (ORCA), a Peruvian marine animal conservation organisation, said that ships using deep water sonar are to blame for the mass deaths.

After studying the corpses of many of the dolphins, it was noticed that they did not bear marks of external damage caused by fishing practices or signs of poisoning.

Instead, researchers found damage in the dolphins' middle ear bones, which is said to be a sign of decompression syndrome.

"We have been noting that the animals were suffering from acute decompression syndrome—that is to say, a violent death produced by an acoustic boom that disorients the animal and produces haemorrhages which cause the animal to end up dying on the beach," said ORCA director Dr Carlos Yaipen.

The damage is said to come from sonic bursts that are produced by deep water sonar signals sometimes used in the search for petroleum. The bursts can damage animals whose communication frequencies fall in the same range.

US federal regulators are curbing an oil and natural gas exploration company from using seismic equipment that sends out underwater pulses along Louisiana's coast until the bottlenose dolphin calving season ends.

ORCA calculates that the phenomenon represents the highest number of beached dolphins recorded anywhere in the world in the last decade.

> *"Regulations require the Navy to implement measures designed to protect and minimize effects to marine mammals."*

# Proper Guidelines Can Protect Marine Mammals from the Effects of Sonar

*National Oceanic and Atmospheric Administration*

*The National Oceanic and Atmospheric Administration (NOAA) is a federal agency dedicated to monitoring the condition of the oceans and atmosphere. In the following viewpoint, NOAA argues that the regulations issued to the US Navy will significantly reduce the harmful effect on marine mammals of navy sonar training. NOAA states that it does not anticipate the navy training to have any impact on fish stock. The regulations, according to NOAA, include establishing safety zones around navy vessels, minimizing specific training known to endanger marine mammals, such as torpedo exercises, educating navy personnel about marine mammal habitats, and monitoring plans to ensure adherence to these regulations.*

As you read, consider the following questions:

1. According to the author, what injuries may the sonar used by the navy cause in marine mammals?

National Oceanic and Atmospheric Administration, "NOAA Gives Navy Marine Mammal Protection Measures for Sonar Training," January 23, 2009. www.noaanews.noaa.gov.

2. According to the NOAA, where does the navy have to establish marine mammal safety zones?

3. In the author's opinion, how long has the navy been conducting sonar training?

NOAA's [National Oceanic and Atmospheric Administration's] Fisheries Service has issued regulations and a letter of authorization to the U.S. Navy that includes measures to protect marine mammals while conducting Atlantic fleet active sonar training off the Atlantic coast and in the Gulf of Mexico. The regulations require the Navy to implement measures designed to protect and minimize effects to marine mammals.

Along with issuing these regulations, NOAA will undertake a comprehensive review of all mitigation measures applicable to the use of sonar and will report to the Council on Environmental Quality regarding the results of this review within 120 days.

## What the Regulations Stipulate

These regulations, in effect for five years, govern the incidental take [killing] of marine mammals during the Navy's training activities, include required mitigation and monitoring measures, and require annual letters of authorization. The letters of authorization, which are required for the Navy to legally conduct their activities, provide the Navy with the terms and conditions of the marine mammal mitigation measures, and requires annual reports, and Navy review of their activities to show they do not result in more numerous effects or more severe harm to marine mammals than were originally analyzed or authorized.

The Navy requested authorization under the Marine Mammal Protection Act because the mid-frequency sound generated by tactical active sonar may affect the behavior of some marine mammals or cause a temporary loss of their hearing.

# Collateral Damage Must Be Expected

NOAA's Fisheries Service does not expect the exercises to result in serious injury or death to marine mammals and is requiring the Navy to use mitigation measures intended to avoid injury or death. However, in a small number of cases, exposure to sonar in certain circumstances has been associated with the stranding of some marine mammals, and some injury or death potentially could occur despite the best efforts of the Navy. Therefore, the regulations and the letter allow for a small number of incidental injuries to marine mammals.

NOAA's Fisheries Service has determined that these effects would have a negligible impact on the species or stocks involved.

Under the regulations and the letter, the Navy must follow mitigation measures to minimize effects on marine mammals, including:

- establishing marine mammal safety zones around each vessel using sonar, and using Navy observers to shut down sonar operations if marine mammals are seen within these designated safety zones;

- implementing a stranding response plan that includes a training shutdown provision in certain circumstances (with special circumstances for North Atlantic right whales) and a memorandum of agreement to allow the Navy to contribute in-kind services to NOAA's Fisheries Service if the agency has to conduct a stranding response and investigation;

- minimizing helicopter dipping sonar and object detection exercises in the North Atlantic right whale critical habitat in the southeast Atlantic Ocean from December through March;

- using several cautionary measures to minimize impacts from torpedo exercises conducted in the North Atlantic right whale critical habitat in the northeast Atlantic Ocean;

- using designated planning awareness areas to raise awareness of Navy personnel and lessen impacts in designated productive marine mammal habitat;

- using several cautionary measures to minimize the likelihood of ship strikes of North Atlantic right whales.

These measures should minimize the potential for injury or death and significantly reduce the number of marine mammals exposed to levels of sound likely to cause temporary loss of hearing.

## A Monitoring Plan Is in Place

NOAA's Fisheries Service and the Navy worked to develop a robust monitoring plan to use independent, trained and experienced aerial and vessel-based marine mammal observers (as well as Navy watch standers) and passive acoustic monitoring to help better understand how marine mammals respond to various levels of sound and to assess the effectiveness of mitigation measures. The implementation of this monitoring plan is included as a requirement of the regulations and the letter.

The Navy has been conducting training exercises, including the use of mid-frequency sonar, in the Atlantic Ocean for more than 40 years. Exercises range from large, three week-long strike group training exercises using multiple submarines, ships and aircraft to two-to-three-day unit level training, consisting of several multi-hour exercises designed to target specific skills or weapons systems, such as object detection or helicopter dipping sonar.

| "*The number of dead dolphins found stranded on the coast close to the spill had dramatically increased.*"

# Oil Spills Cause Long-Term Health Issues for Marine Mammals

*Peter Beaumont*

*Peter Beaumont is a foreign affairs editor at the* Observer, *a British newspaper. In the following viewpoint, Beaumont reports on a study by the National Oceanic and Atmospheric Administration on dolphins living in the Gulf of Mexico near the April 2010 British Petroleum (BP) Deepwater Horizon oil spill. Many of the dolphins in the study suffered health problems such as weight loss, anemia, and lung and liver disease, facing grim chances for long-term survival, according to the study, Beaumont reports. The severity of the oil spill damaged even usually unaffected organisms such as deepwater coral and marshland animals, says Beaumont.*

As you read, consider the following questions:

1. According to Beaumont, what potential effects can be expected due to the hormone deficiency detected in the studied dolphins?

2. In the author's opinion, what factors contributed to the damage the oil spill caused to coral?

3. As stated by Beaumont, which marshland animals have also been affected by the oil spill?

A new study of dolphins living close to the site of North America's worst ever oil spill—the BP Deepwater Horizon catastrophe two years ago [in 2010]—has established serious health problems afflicting the marine mammals.

The report, commissioned by the National Oceanic and Atmospheric Administration [NOAA], found that many of the 32 dolphins studied were underweight, anaemic and suffering from lung and liver disease, while nearly half had low levels of a hormone that helps the mammals deal with stress as well as regulate their metabolism and immune systems.

More than 200 million gallons of crude oil flowed from the well after a series of explosions on 20 April 2010, which killed 11 workers. The spill contaminated the Gulf of Mexico and its coastline in what President Barack Obama called America's worst environmental disaster.

The research follows the publication of several scientific studies into insect populations on the nearby Gulf coastline and into the health of deepwater coral populations, which all suggest that the environmental impact of the five-month-long spill may have been far worse than previously appreciated.

Another study confirmed that zooplankton—the micro-scopic organisms at the bottom of the ocean food chain—had also been contaminated with oil. Indeed, photographs issued last month [February 2012] of wetland coastal areas show continued contamination, with some areas still devoid of veg-etation.

## Dolphin Deaths Have Increased

The study of the dolphins in Barataria Bay, off the coast of Louisiana, followed two years in which the number of dead dolphins found stranded on the coast close to the spill had

## Oil Spill Strands Hundreds of Dolphins

Scientists do not know how many distinct dolphin populations there were in the Gulf before the spill. They generally agree that the 700 dolphins that have stranded in the last two years represent only a fraction of the animals that have died in the same period of time. But what fraction? Wildlife biologists often work on the premise that for every carcass that washes ashore, there are more than 10 dolphins whose bodies are never recovered.

*Suzanne Goldenberg,* The Guardian *(Manchester, UK),*
*April 12, 2012.*

dramatically increased. Although all but one of the 32 dolphins were still alive when the study ended, lead researcher Lori Schwacke said survival prospects for many were grim, adding that the hormone deficiency—while not definitively linked to the oil spill—was "consistent with oil exposure to other mammals".

Schwacke told a Colorado-based publication last week: "This was truly an unprecedented event—there was little existing data that would indicate what effects might be seen specifically in dolphins—or other cetaceans [whales and dolphins]—exposed to oil for a prolonged period of time."

The NOAA study has been reported at the same time as two other studies suggesting that the long-term environmental effects of the Deepwater Horizon spill may have been far more profound than previously thought.

## Corals Covered by Plumes of Oil

A study of deep ocean corals seven miles from the spill source jointly funded by the NOAA and BP has found dead and dying corals coated "in brown gunk". Deepwater corals are not usually affected in oil spills, but the depth and temperatures involved in the spill appear to have been responsible for creating plumes of oil particles deep under the ocean surface, which are blamed for the unprecedented damage.

Charles Fisher, one of the scientists who jointly described the impact as unprecedented, said he believed the colony had been contaminated by a plume from the ruptured well which would have affected other organisms. "The corals are long-living and don't move. That is why we were able to identify the damage but you would have expected it to have had an impact on other larger animals that were exposed to it."

Chemical analysis of oil found on the dying coral showed that it came from the Deepwater Horizon spill.

## Battles Rage over the Cleanup Bill

The latest surveys of the damage to the marine environment come amid continued legal wrangling between the US and BP over the bill for the clean-up. BP said the US government was withholding evidence that would show the oil spill from the well in the Gulf of Mexico was smaller than claimed. Last week [the end of March 2012] BP, which has set aside $37bn [billion] (£23bn) to pay for costs associated with the disaster, went to court in Louisiana to demand access to thousands of documents that it says the Obama administration is suppressing.

The US government is still pursuing a case against BP despite a deal the company reached at the beginning of March with the largest group of private claimants. That $7.8bn deal, however, does not address "significant damages" to the environment after the spill for which BP has not admitted liability. And it has not only been the immediate marine environment that has been affected. A study of insect populations in the coastal marshes affected by the catastrophe has also identified significant impact.

## Damages Extend to Wetlands

Linda Hooper-Bui of Louisiana State University found that some kinds of insect and spider were far less numerous than before. "Every single time we go out there, the Pollyanna [someone who is unduly optimistic] part of me thinks, 'Now we're going to measure recovery'," she said. "Then I get out there and say: 'Whaaat?'"

She had expected that one group of arthropods [animals with an external skeleton, such as insects, spiders, and crayfish] might be hit hard while others recovered, but her work, still incomplete, shows a large downturn among many kinds. "We never thought it would be this big, this widespread," she said.

For its part BP has claimed in a recent statement that it has worked hard to fulfil its responsibility to clean up after the spill. "From the beginning, BP stepped up to meet our obligations to the communities in the Gulf Coast region, and we've worked hard to deliver on that commitment for nearly two years," BP chief executive Bob Dudley declared recently.

| "Why are salmon farmers in Canada, Chile, Scotland and Norway allowed to kill marine mammals and then export farmed salmon to the United States?"

# Salmon from Countries That Allow Fish Farmers to Kill Marine Mammals Should Be Boycotted

*David Ainsley, Kurt Beardslee, et al.*

*David Ainsley of Sealife Adventures in Scotland, along with representatives from sea mammal organizations worldwide, co-signed a letter to the US undersecretary of commerce for oceans and atmosphere regarding the killing of seals and sea lions at salmon farms.*

*In the following viewpoint, the authors urge US retailers to boycott salmon from farms that kill marine mammals. The authors assert that killing marine mammals in Canadian, Scots, and Chilean salmon farms is common practice. The killing of these mammals is not an economic necessity, they contend, but unnecessary animal cruelty banned under the US Marine Mammal Protection Act.*

David Ainsley, Kurt Beardslee, et al., "Killing of Seals and Sea Lions at Salmon Farms—Breach of MMPA," Letter to Dr. Jane Lubchenco, Under Secretary of Commerce for Oceans and Atmosphere, October 5, 2011. http://www.dukeschowderhouse.com.

As you read, consider the following questions:

1. According to the authors, how many seals and sea lions were killed in Canada between 1989 and 2000?

2. According to Ainsley et al., what could salmon farms that kill marine mammals install to keep such predators away?

3. As described by the authors, what are some of the methods Maine salmon farms use to keep marine mammal predators away?

We, the undersigned, write regarding the lethal nature of salmon farming operations and a breach of the U.S. Marine Mammal Protection Act (MMPA). Recent evidence in Canada and Scotland in particular provides damning evidence of the deliberate and systematic shooting of seals and sea lions—including the killing of Steller sea lions (protected under Species at Risk Act in Canada and listed as threatened under the U.S. Endangered Species Act) earlier this year [2011] in the Clayoquot Sound UNESCO [United Nations Educational, Scientific, and Cultural Organization] Biosphere Reserve in British Columbia. . . .

In 2010, U.S. retailer Target announced that it would no longer sell farmed salmon from its stores. Until salmon farmers stop shooting seals and sea lions we urge other retailers to follow Target's lead. Please don't allow marine mammals to be used as a target for shooting practice.

## Seal/Sea Lion–Friendly Salmon

The U.S. Government has a unique opportunity via the MMPA to step in and demand seal/sea lion–friendly salmon (following on from 'dolphin-friendly tuna'). In 2005, a legal opinion obtained by the National Environmental Trust on 'Prohibition on the Importation of Fish from Salmon Farms Where Seals Are Shot' concluded that:

"The MMPA provides a strong and directly applicable legal tool to address this problem. Fish caught from the salmon farms operated by companies in foreign countries that engage in lethal deterrence is subject to the importation ban of section 102(c)(3). In addition to the clear prohibition against importation of fish from salmon farms where seals are shot under section 102(c)(3), it is possible that this activity may fall within the scope of section 101(a)(2) of the MMPA and the related import restrictions."

Based on the continued killing of marine mammals, we therefore ask that imports of farmed salmon from those countries and companies sponsoring and sanctioning lethal controls be excluded from the U.S. market. We ask that the U.S. send a strong signal that the killing of marine mammals will no longer be tolerated, especially in relation to salmon farming operations which may market their products in the U.S. as 'organic', 'sustainable' and 'responsible'. Chile, Canada, Norway and Scotland are the four largest export countries to the U.S. market—and in the first six months of 2011, USA imports of all salmon products totalized 132,870 tonnes worth US$1,175 million.

## Seals and Sea Lions Slaughtered

In Canada, the slaughter of seals on the East coast is common knowledge but on the West coast in British Columbia the killing of seals and sea lions including the protected Steller sea lion by salmon farms has received less public attention. Data published by the Department of Fisheries and Oceans Canada reported the killing of 6,243 seals and sea lions at salmon farms between 1989–2000. The Canadian Government report—'Salmon Farm–Pinniped Interactions in British Columbia: An analysis of predator control; its justification and alternative approaches'—stated that:

"It should be noted that US legislation and regulations may have implications for fish farms in Canada. The US

MMPA of 1972 as Amended, Sec. 102 (c) (3) states that: '[It is unlawful to import into the US] any fish, whether fresh, frozen, or otherwise prepared .... This would seem to indicate that fish harvested from fish farms in a manner that would not be permitted in the US (by shooting seals and sea lions) might not be able to be sold in the US markets, but a legal interpretation is required to evaluate this".

Data for 2001 to 2010 is not readily available but new data published by the Department of Fisheries and Oceans Canada for the first three months of 2011 reveals licensed killing of marine mammals as well as 'accidental drownings' on salmon farms in British Columbia. *The Vancouver Sun* reported (16th September [2011]) that:

"Between January and March, 37 harbour seals, 141 California sea lions and two Steller sea lions, which are of 'special concern' under the federal Species at Risk Act, were shot and killed at fish farms, according to data posted on the DFO [Department of Fisheries and Oceans, Canada] website. Three more harbour seals and a California sea lion drowned at the farms within the same period." ...

## Salmon Farms Are Killing Fields

An article—"A Practice That Is Impossible to Defend"—published last week (30th September [2011]) in *The Courier-Islander* newspaper in Canada included:

"Considering that these corporate salmon farms are camped in the middle of a marine thoroughfare for migrating mammals—and wild fish, too—the obvious way to ensure 'zero lethal interaction' would be to get their net-pens out of the ocean. ... Removing their net-pens from the natural habitat of unmanageable mammals while suffering the deprivation of less profitability must be a much more painful prospect than enduring the anguish of distributing sea lice, polluting, and killing seals and sea lions. And how many seals and sea lions? DFO's numbers are sobering. Of the 13 years reported,

1997 was the worst year for seals when 550 were killed—500 were common at this time. The worst year for sea lions was 2000 when 250 were shot because they weren't 'intelligent' enough to know that salmon farms are lethal. For anyone concerned with this bloodshed, the consolation is that those were only the most bloody years. The killing of 180 animals in 2011—plus the four that drowned—is excused by the rise in their population, a defence that uses plenitude to justify slaughter."

An Editorial—'A Smoking Gun Is a Smoking Gun'—also published last week (30th September [2011]) in *The Courier-Islander* stated:

"Between January and March of 2011 141 California sea lions, 37 harbour seals and two Stellar sea lions were killed by the fish farming industry because the animals were a problem around the open net cage fish sites. That's 180 animals in 90 days. Two a day . . . . Now, however, they are not just farm sites, they are killing fields".

Writing in *The Westerly News* (29th September [2011]), Don Staniford asked:

"Does anyone else feel that shooting seals and sea lions in a UNESCO Biosphere Reserve is simply wrong? . . . The United Nations—which awarded Clayoquot Sound its status as a UNESCO Biosphere Reserve—should step in to keep the peace and stop the killing of hundreds of seals and sea lions each year." . . .

## Buying Farmed Salmon Helps Kill Seals

In Scotland, too, the killing of seals has recently hit the headlines with licences to kill 1,298 seals issued for 2011 by the Scottish Government. Andy Ottaway, Director of the Seal Protection Action, said: "An average of over three seals shot every single day is too high a price to pay for Scottish Salmon. . . . The Scottish Government and Salmon industry can and must implement better industry practices and technologies to end these seal killings which leave an indelible stain on the international image of both Scotland and Scottish salmon products".

*The Sun* reported in February this year [2011] under the headline "'Boycott Salmon' over seal killings" that: "Most of the licences have been given to fish farmers to stop seals breaking through nets to eat their salmon." Last night John Robins, of animal rights groups Animal Concern and Save Our Seals Fund, said: "I am furious that the Scottish Government has passed a death sentence on over a thousand seals. The Government have lied to us over this. They said seal shooting would only be allowed as a last resort. Marine Scotland have made it official—if you buy Scottish salmon you pay for bullets to shoot seals. We are calling on the public to boycott Scottish salmon." A Scottish Government spokesman said: "The shooting of seals should always be a last resort."

However, the shooting of seals in Scotland is being used as a first not last resort with most salmon farms not using antipredator nets. John F. Robins, Save Our Seals Fund, wrote in *The Herald* newspaper in May 2011: "The Scottish Government has admitted that not one salmon farm was visited prior to being granted a licence to shoot seals and Government figures show that 80% of the floating factory-fish farms given licences to shoot seals do not have anti-predator nets. Shooting seals is being used as a first resort, not a last resort".

In August 2011, *Shetland News* reported that: "SSPCA officers raided Hoganess Salmon, near Walls, on Shetland's west side after reports that seals had been killed illegally. They were supported by the local police and staff from Scottish Natural Heritage".

## Killing Seals Can Be Avoided

*For Argyll* reported in March 2011 that the slaughter involved the shooting of pregnant seals in the breeding season and stated:

"Why are salmon farmers shooting seals? Seals are intelligent animals and if they get the opportunity and there is only one net between them and the salmon they will, as David Ainsley of Sealife Adventures says: 'push against that net and take lumps out of the salmon.'"

So why can it be said that is it unnecessary to shoot seals? Because properly designed, installed and maintained *double* netted cages keep seals and salmon separated. To avoid drowning seals, otters, porpoise and birds, the outer nets must be of the same material and mesh size as the inner nets. And why does the industry not use double nets? Cost, of course. It is obviously cheaper to use single nets and bullets. But the industry is expanding, profitable and can afford to install these double nets.

Why, in an Act whose own guidance declaims that shooting seals should be a last resort, is there no obligation to use double nets and no penalty for failing to do so? Shooting seals as a last resort means that the farms must have tried the most effective non-lethal method (i.e. double nets) *before* they are granted a licence to shoot seals. But 80% of the salmon farms now granted licenses do not have double nets. We do not know why the government has failed to follow its own guidelines but we must act to try to get these licenses rescinded and the cull stopped. . . .

## Sea Lion Deaths in Chile

In Chile, too, there is recent evidence of the deaths of sea lions due to salmon farm nets. *Wildlife Extra* reported in 2010 that: "The animals get caught in the protective nets surrounding the salmon farms when young and, even if they manage to free themselves, parts of the nets often remain stuck to the sea lions and suffocate them as they grow".

In 2008, *The Patagonia Times* reported: "An Aysén tourism operator recently sent a letter to maritime authorities in Puerto Cisnes describing a dead sea lion discovered on Valle

## Canadian Salmon Farmers Must Kill Seals

In Canada, salmon farmers are obliged by law to kill harbour seals, California sea lions, and Steller sea lions. In 2000, a mass grave containing 15 sea lions was discovered in the Clayoquot Sound UNESCO Biosphere Reserve. Over 5,000 sea lions and seals have been killed since 1990 by fish farmers in British Columbia.

*Pure Salmon Campaign, 2008.*
*www.puresalmon.org.*

Marta beach," the environmental NGO [nongovernmental organization] Ecoceanos reported this week. "The body had two (12 calibre) bullet holes similar to the other 23 sea lion bodies found on the same beach over the past four years," the letter read. The letter contained photographs of the dead animal, which was found with the remnants of a rope tied around its neck. Presumably the person who killed the sea lion tied rocks to it in order to sink the body. "If one considers that only a small number of the sea lion bodies come back to the surface after being sunk with rock-filled bags, it's clear that this practice (of killing sea lions) has not stopped despite numerous complaints," the letter went on to say.

According to Terram (a Chilean NGO), thousands of sea lions in Chile, mostly males, die each year near salmon farms, shot by guards ordered to "kill any spotted around salmon farms".

Canada, Scotland and Chile are not the only countries where salmon farmers kill seals. In New Zealand in July this year it was reported by the *Marlborough Express* that a salmon farmer "admitted charges of possessing an offensive weapon, a galvanised steel pole, in a public place at Ohau Point, and wilfully ill-treating 23 seals by clubbing them to death".

## Use the Law to Protect Sea Mammals

In Maine, salmon farmers are prohibited from killing seals and sea lions under the MMPA. An article from 1996, for example, reported that:

"Salmon growers in Maine employ a variety of predator control measures—netting systems, underwater acoustic devices and pyrotechnics—but no battery of protections seems to be 100% effective. In the past, those seals who could defeat deterrence strategies would be targeted for lethal removal. Recent amendments to the Marine Mammal Protection Act (MMPA), however now prohibit the killing of depredating [hunting] seals".

We also note a 2003 report from SeaWeb which stated that: "Under the Marine Mammal Protection Act, salmon farmers in the United States are prohibited from shooting seals". And a press release from the Pure Salmon Campaign in 2006 which stated that:

"Almost all farmed salmon is raised in open ocean pens. Consequently, seals and sea lions swim around these large nets looking for an easy meal. Salmon farmers routinely shoot and kill these marine mammals, animals that are strictly protected in the U.S."

The Pure Salmon Campaign also stated in 2007 that: "The Marine Mammal Protection Act in the United States forbids the harassment or killing of marine mammals and the U.S. can forbid the import of any product resulting in the death of marine mammals".

So, if the United States prohibits the shooting of seals and sea lions by salmon farmers in Maine or Washington State then why are salmon farmers in Canada, Chile, Scotland and Norway allowed to kill marine mammals and then export farmed salmon to the United States?

In view of ongoing evidence of marine mammal killings, we respectfully ask that the U.S. Government invoke the MMPA and prohibit the import of farmed salmon from salmon farms in British Columbia, Scotland and Chile.

"*There is a conservation imperative to reduce human-caused mortality of marine mammals in the many areas where proper assessment is lacking and governance is inadequate.*"

# Hunting of Marine Mammals Needs to Be Regulated

*Doug O'Harra*

*Doug O'Harra is an Alaskan writer and science journalist. In the following viewpoint, he claims that marine mammal consumption is on the rise worldwide. While marine mammal hunting has been a tradition in Alaska and Japan for generations, he explains, it is a new phenomenon in many other countries, fueled by declining catches of other fish, international population growth, and bycatch issues. Hunters of Alaskan marine mammals cooperate with scientists and conservationists to develop hunting practices and limits that ensure the long-term health of the marine mammal populations, O'Harra reports, and encourages other nations to follow this lead.*

As you read, consider the following questions:

1. What does the author claim is the percentage of marine mammals taken for food?

2. According to O'Harra, which country consumes the most marine animals?

3. In the author's opinion, why did Point Lay villagers receive an award?

Killing marine mammals for food has increased over the past few decades worldwide—often by tropical zone fishermen netting animals in situations without controls to avoid overharvests—according to a new study that examined 900 sources of information across the globe.

"It is now clear that human consumption of marine mammals is geographically widespread, taxonomically diverse [i.e., a variety of species], and often of uncertain sustainability," scientists Martin Robards and Randall Reeves wrote in a review published this month [December 2011] in the journal *Biological Conservation*. "Since 1990, people in at least 114 countries have consumed one or more of at least 87 marine mammal species."

Among the findings: The number of countries reporting marine mammal consumption rose from 107 to 125 during the past 30 years, with an overall increase of 12 species, most of them small cetaceans like dolphins and porpoises.

"Our review highlights an escalation in utilization of small cetaceans caught in conjunction with fishing activities since 1970, a form of fishing-up-the-food-chain," they wrote. "Where consumption relates to food security and poverty, we found evidence of deliberate killing of animals caught both deliberately and accidentally in fishing gear."

Only 6 percent of the 1,400 marine species taken for food are marine mammals (most are fish), but the trend suggests that officials need to take action before more marine mammal populations are depleted or wiped out, according to an editorial titled "Who Eats Sea Meat?" in the same issue of the journal.

"Considering the media attention given to stopping the hunting of whales (large cetaceans) for human consumption, it may come as a surprise that people are eating more marine mammal species than ever before," wrote Mark Costello of University of Auckland and C. Scott Baker at Oregon State University. "It is time for national governments and the international community to recognize this threat and begin seeking solutions . . ."

## Native Peoples Hunt Marine Mammals

The study also outlined North American marine mammal use, much of it in occurring along Alaska and Canada coasts by Native people engaged in subsistence. Some 17 species have been taken by U.S. hunters since 1990, including bowhead and gray whales, beluga whales, seals, sea lions and walruses.

A goal of the study was to put Alaska Native harvests in an international context, according to Robards, who conducted the research while working at the federal Marine Mammal Commission. Alaska marine mammal kills, especially during the traditional hunts for bowhead whales in the Arctic often gets outsized media attention.

"We were surprised to find so much marine mammal use elsewhere," said Robards, now with the Wildlife Conservation Society in Fairbanks and formerly with the U.S. Geological Survey in Anchorage.

Alaska Natives and other indigenous peoples of the Arctic have always relied on seals, sea lions, whales and small cetaceans like beluga whales to feed their families. These harvests often form the backbone of traditional life in Alaska coastal villages, providing sustenance that goes far beyond filling bellies.

But the modern Alaskan model—where Native hunters work with biologists to set harvest quotas and ensure sustained yield—isn't how local hunters and fishermen do it on many other continents.

## Subsistence Hunting Is Unregulated

"While in Alaska/Canada there's increasing collaboration between tribes, co-management bodies, and agencies to conserve marine mammals being used for subsistence," Robards said, "the use of marine mammals in the tropics is frequently unregulated and of very questionable sustainability."

In their study, Robards and Reeves distinguished between killing marine mammals in "targeted" hunts and killing them after the animals were caught in fishing nets or entrapped by ice. They noted that people salvaged marine mammals found dead or unintentionally killed.

"Our estimates of the number of carcasses used for consumption suggest that in at least 27 countries, hundreds or thousands of marine mammals provide food for human consumption each year," they wrote. "Many of the countries with the greatest use of marine mammals for food are at least partly in high northern latitudes. Japan is by far the largest consumer of marine mammals based on the annual number of animals killed for consumption."

Increasing marine mammal takes—especially dolphins and porpoises intentionally killed after capture in fishing nets—can be partly explained by the proliferation of modern synthetic nets, the authors explained. The global decline of fish catches, combined with population growth, poverty and hunger for meat, has also driven the trend.

In many places, biologists know very little about local population numbers, making it all but impossible to determine safe harvest levels.

"Consequently," they wrote, "there is a conservation imperative to reduce human-caused mortality of marine mammals in the many areas where proper assessment is lacking and governance is inadequate."

## Alaskan Hunters Work with Scientists

In Alaska, Native hunters now work closely with biologists, sharing data and following harvest guidelines.

"For Alaska readers, I have really wanted to emphasize that there's a real maturation of the collaborative work between tribes, scientists, and agencies," Robards told Dispatch. "It's not just about eating the animals in Alaska—the communities and co-management bodies are actively involved in discussions around shipping and other development activities in the Arctic to ensure that the marine mammals are conserved."

One dramatic example cited by Robards came in the fall of 2010, when tens of thousands of walruses hauled out on a Chukchi Sea barrier island in response to the lack of sea ice. Villagers from Point Lay took control of the situation on the ground and made sure that the animals were not disturbed. The U.S. Fish and Widlife Service later recognized the village with an "Outstanding Partner" award.

"Point Lay has a distinguished history of working closely with wildlife scientists, especially on beluga and bowhead whales. In this instance the entire community also took the initiative to effectively demonstrate respect and provide respite for the thousands of weary Pacific walruses resting near the village," the agency said in a release.

Canada and Australia also deploy Alaska-style co-management to oversee and regulate marine mammal harvests, Robards said. Unlike Arctic Native people, who target dozens of marine mammal species, Australian indigenous people harvest only the dugong [a type of manatee].

# Periodical and Internet Sources Bibliography

*The following articles have been chosen to supplement the diverse views presented in this chapter.*

| | |
|---|---|
| *Columbia Basin Bulletin* | "Sea Lions Find Their Way Above Bonneville Dam; 'Raising Hell' in Tribal Subsistence Fishery," May 18, 2012. www.cbbulletin.com. |
| Nancy Gaines | "See Seals? Great Whites Not Far Behind," *Gloucester (MA) Times*, July 18, 2012. |
| Melissa Gaskill | "In Its First Life, an Oil Platform; in Its Next, a Reef?," *New York Times*, June 17, 2012. |
| Phil Gast | "Whales, Dolphins Die as Navy Trains," *Keene (NH) Sentinel*, May 12, 2012. www.sentinel source.com. |
| Taryn Kiekow | "The International Whaling Commission: The Good, the Bad and the Ugly," *Switchboard* (blog), July 6, 2012. www.switchboard.nrdc.org. |
| Tafline Laylin | "Namibia's 'Cruel' Seal Hunt Sparks Calls for Tourism Boycott," *The Ecologist*, April 12, 2012. |
| Steve Maley | "The Environmentally Friendly Oil Platform," Red State, June 19, 2012. www.redstate.com. |
| Sandy McElhaney | "Scapegoating + Bad Math = Devastation for Federally Protected Sea Lions at the Bonneville Dam," Sea Shepherd, April 2, 2012. www .seashepherd.org. |
| Mary O'Malley, Hannah Medd, and Samantha Whitcraft | "Shark Fin Trade Myths and Truths: Bycatch," Shark Savers, January 27, 2012. www.shark savers.org. |
| Onearth | "Arctic Meltdown, Mammals on the Move, Oil Rig Ecosystems," June 18, 2012. www.onearth .org. |

# For Further Discussion

## Chapter 1

1.  Carl Zimmer argues that the increased levels of ocean acidification are due to human behavior and if not counteracted may cause the extinction of species. Christopher Monckton claims that the current levels of ocean acidification must be attributed to natural causes, which, by extension, means that a possible extinction of species is a natural development as well. Using the viewpoints to inform your answer, should strategies to counteract ocean acidification in order to avoid the extinction of species be devised, or should the oceans be allowed to adjust to the increased levels of acidification naturally? Explain.

2.  Humberto Fontova is in favor of offshore oil drilling because it ensures energy independence for the United States and thus ensures the nation's economic health. The Natural Resources Defense Council argues that offshore drilling does not necessarily guarantee economic independence, as the danger of oil spills in fact threatens the economy of coastal communities. Which view do you agree with more? Are effects of an oil spill on the environment and its effects on the economy two isolated issues? If so, is it possible to value one over the other? If you believe the effects are related, explain how.

## Chapter 2

1.  Michael Conathan argues that by prescribing local and federal offices to work toward a common goal, the National Ocean Policy will ensure overall ocean health and thus overall economic health. Pete Winn argues the opposite: A federal policy will hamper local fisheries and businesses with unnecessary laws and regulations that ultimately create nothing but stifling bureaucracy.

Considering these two viewpoints, do you think states and municipalities should be allowed to operate according to their own laws and regulations in this regard? Why or why not? What advantages or disadvantages are there to federal laws as opposed to local or state laws?

2. Chris Maser argues that marine protected areas are necessary to ensure ocean biodiversity, while Dan Bacher claims that marine protected areas are an economic burden to coastal communities. Using the arguments in these viewpoints, do you think that ensuring biodiversity and ensuring economic health are mutually exclusive, or does one depend on the other? Explain.

3. The Ocean Health Index proposes to rate the health of local ocean patches with a single number. Having read the viewpoint by Ben Halpern and colleagues, do you think that grading ocean health with a single number can be a touchstone for discussing strategies that counteract very specific and potentially varied local issues, or do you think that a single grade will gloss over details of local circumstances? Use arguments from the viewpoint to support your opinion.

## Chapter 3

1. Carl Safina argues that the concept of maximum sustainable yield is based on the false assumption that the ocean produces a surplus, when in fact any supposed surplus is in reality a vital part of the marine food chain. The European Commission claims that the concept of maximum sustainable yield can be used successfully if the most vulnerable species in any given stock becomes its basis. Weighing these two viewpoints against each other, should the notion of maximum sustainable yield be abandoned in favor of other practices? Why or why not?

2. The Ocean Conservancy argues that offshore fish farming poses unacceptable risks to wild fish stock. Listing argu-

ments both for and against aquaculture, Harold F. Upton and Eugene H. Buck contend that aquaculture equipment and technology could be improved and adjusted to minimize the effect on wild fish and stock and marine mammals. Using arguments from these viewpoints, do you think that fish farming could be a solution to the ever-increasing demand for fish for consumption? Why or why not?

## Chapter 4

1. KiPNews holds navy sonar responsible for the death of marine mammals, while the National Oceanic and Atmospheric Administration, a federal government agency, claims that its regulations protect marine mammals from harm while allowing the navy to conduct vital experiments. Given that sonar is not only used by the navy, but also by local municipalities and oil companies in searching for profitable and safe oilfields, which argument do you find more compelling? Why? Do you think that the effect of sonar on marine mammals should have an impact on whether it is used? Why or why not?

2. Peter Beaumont argues that the 2010 BP oil spill caused obvious and long-lasting damage to the Gulf Coast environment. Having read this viewpoint, do you think that the demand for energy supplied by offshore oil supersedes the need of marine mammals for a healthy ocean environment? Is protecting marine life reason enough to abandon offshore drilling? Why or why not?

# Organizations to Contact

*The editors have compiled the following list of organizations concerned with the issues debated in this book. The descriptions are derived from materials provided by the organizations. All have publications or information available for interested readers. The list was compiled on the date of publication of the present volume; names, addresses, phone and fax numbers, and email and Internet addresses may change. Be aware that many organizations take several weeks or longer to respond to inquiries, so allow as much time as possible.*

**American Cetacean Society**
PO Box 1391, San Pedro, CA   90733
(310) 546-6279 • fax: (310) 548-6950
e-mail: acsoffice@acsonline.org
website: http://acsonline.org

The American Cetacean Society is a volunteer organization working to protect whales, dolphins, porpoises, and their habitats through public education, research grants, and conservation actions. Its publications include fact sheets and reports as well as the society's semiannual research journal *Whalewatcher*.

**Atlantic Marine Aquaculture Center**
University of New Hampshire, Durham, NH   03824
(603) 862-3685
e-mail: dolores.leonard@unh.edu
website: http://ooa.unh.edu

The Atlantic Marine Aquaculture Center is a federally funded research institution aiming to provide the research and development necessary to stimulate an environmentally sustainable offshore aquaculture industry in New England and nationwide. The center studies stock enhancement as a tool to revive wild-capture fisheries. The website's publication link includes project briefs, reports, and journal articles by the center's science staff.

## Blue Frontier Campaign

PO Box 19367, Washington, DC   20036
(202) 387-8030
e-mail: info@bluefront.org
website: www.bluefront.org

Founder David Helvang, author of *Blue Frontier—Saving America's Living Seas,* started this environmental group in 2003 to promote public awareness of coastal and ocean preservation. Using grassroots campaigns, the organization hopes to influence policies and national decision making that advocate sustainability. The group's website provides access to a rich array of articles, book excerpts, and commentary, as well as its e-newsletter *Blue Notes.*

## Environmental Defense Fund (EDF)

1875 Connecticut Ave. NW, Suite 600, Washington, DC   20009
(800) 684-3322
e-mail: members@environmentaldefense.org
website: www.edf.org

The Environmental Defense Fund is a group of scientists, economists, attorneys, and other professionals with the common goal of preserving the environment by finding lasting practical solutions for today's environmental issues. The nonprofit organization is set apart by its innovative multidisciplinary approach. The EDF publishes an annual report and provides access to recent and archived articles on current fishing, aquaculture, ocean, and global warming issues on its website.

## Greenpeace International

Ottho Heldringstraat 5, Amsterdam, AZ   1066
  The Netherlands
+31 20 718 2000 • fax: +31 20 718 2002
e-mail: supporter.services.int@greenpeace.org
website: www.greenpeace.org

Greenpeace is an independent global campaigning organization that acts to change attitudes and behavior in order to protect and conserve the environment and to promote peace.

Ocean and wildlife preservation is among the organization's goals. Using controversial direct-action techniques, and a website publishing fact sheets on ocean and other environmental concerns, Greenpeace strives to educate the public on current environmental issues and policies. Greenpeace publishes reports, as well as a blog, on issues pertaining to environmental issues and policies.

**Marine Fish Conservation Network**
600 Pennsylvania Ave. SE, Suite 210, Washington, DC   20003
(202) 543-5509
website: www.conservefish.org

The Marine Fish Conservation Network advances national policies in support of healthy oceans and productive fisheries. Among other things, the organization strives to promote sustainable fishing practices and management in an effort to conserve marine ecosystems and protect essential fish habitats by eliminating overfishing and preventing bycatch. The website's "Catch of the Day" link includes articles and editorials on current marine conservation issues.

**National Aquaculture Association**
PO Box 1647, Pine Bluff, AR   71613
(870) 850-7900 • fax: (870) 850-7902
e-mail: naa@thenaa.net
website: www.thenaa.net

The National Aquaculture Association is a trade organization for the aquaculture industry, representing both ocean- and land-based fish-farming operations. The organization strives to promote national programs and policies that further the common interests of the aquaculture industry. The association further fosters cost-effective environmental stewardship and sustainability. Its report *Environmental Stewardship* is accessible on its website.

**National Oceanic and Atmospheric Administration (NOAA)**
1401 Constitution Ave. NW, Room 5128
Washington, DC   20230

e-mail: outreach@noaa.gov
website: www.noaa.gov

The National Oceanic and Atmospheric Administration is a government agency comprising several organizations such as the National Marine Fisheries Service or the National Ocean Service or the National Weather Service. The agency's goal is to educate the public about environmental issues, and it provides services such as daily weather forecasts, severe storm warnings, and climate monitoring to fisheries management, coastal restoration projects, and marine commerce. Almost all NOAA programs are science and research based, and strive to protect life and property and to conserve and protect natural resources.

**Natural Resources Defense Council (NRDC)**
40 W. Twentieth Street, New York, NY   10011
(212) 727-2700 • fax: (212) 727-1773
website: www.nrdc.org

The NRDC is a grassroots environmental-action group aiming to safeguard the earth and the people, plants, and animals inhabiting it. The group focuses on issues such as combating global warming, developing clean energy sources, reviving the world's oceans and defending endangered wildlife to foster a sustainable world. Its work involves education, legislation, and activism. NRDC publishes reports such as *Keeping Oceans Wild: How Marine Reserves Protect Our Living Seas*, as well as the quarterly magazine *OnEarth*.

**The Nature Conservancy**
4245 N. Fairfax Drive, Suite 100, Arlington, VA   22203-1606
(703) 841-5300
website: www.nature.org

The Nature Conservancy is an environmental organization composed of scientists in the United States and thirty-three other countries. The organization partners with governments around the world, as well as with nonprofit organizations and corporations, aiming to conserve the environment. Its collaborative approach is aimed at finding practical solutions so that nature can continue to provide shelter and sustenance upon which animal and human life depends. The organization encourages individual membership and publishes a regular blog as well as papers and articles on its website.

## Ocean Conservancy

1300 Nineteenth Street NW, 8th Floor
Washington, DC   20036
(202) 429-5609
e-mail: membership@oceanconservancy.org
website: www.oceanconservancy.org

Ocean Conservancy aims to empower citizens to take action on behalf of the ocean. Engaging in science-based advocacy, research, and public education, the organization strives to conserve marine fish populations, restore coastal waters, conserve and recover vulnerable marine wildlife, protect ocean ecosystems, and establish ocean wilderness areas. Its quarterly *Ocean Conservancy* is available on the website as are recent fact sheets, articles, and reports.

## SeaWeb

8401 Colesville Road, Suite 500, Silver Spring, MD   20910
(301) 495-9570 • fax: (301) 495-4846
e-mail: contactus@seaweb.org
website: www.seaweb.org

SeaWeb is an international nonprofit organization dedicated to using multimedia methods of communication to influence the way people think about and interact with the oceans. Its mission is to raise awareness of issues pertaining to ocean conservation by bringing together diverse viewpoints that reflect the complexity of marine issues. SeaWeb promotes science- and market-based policy solutions. It offers an international mission statement and annual reports on its website.

## Surfrider Foundation

PO Box 6010, San Clemente, CA   92674-6010
(949) 492-8170 • fax: (949) 492-8142
website: www.surfrider.org

The Surfrider Foundation is a nonprofit organization aiming to protect and enjoy the ocean through an international network of activists. Founded by three surfers in Malibu, California, Surfrider Foundation is a grassroots movement dedicated to conservation, activism, research, and education. Its bimonthly publication *Making Waves* is available on its website, as are news and press releases on current ocean, beach, and coastline issues.

## Whale and Dolphin Conservation Society North America

7 Nelson Street, Plymouth, MA   02360-4044
(888) 699-4253
e-mail: contact@wdcs.org
website: www.wdcs-na.org

The society is an international organization dedicated to the conservation and welfare of all whales, dolphins, and porpoises, collectively known as cetaceans. The society's objectives are to raise awareness and to reduce and ultimately eliminate the continuing threats to cetaceans and their habitats. The society publishes papers, reports, and the newsletter *Whale Watch*. All publications are accessible on its website.

## World Wildlife Fund (WWF)

1250 Twenty-Fourth Street NW
Washington, DC   20090-7180
(202) 293-4800 • fax: (202) 293-9211
website: www.worldwildlife.org

The WWF is a global organization acting locally through a network of offices. The largest privately supported international conservation organization in the world, the WWF is dedicated to protecting the world's wildlife and wildlands. The WWF directs its conservation efforts toward protecting endangered spaces, saving endangered species, and addressing global environmental threats. Its "Wave Forward" web page links web users to fact sheets and articles on current issues related to marine life, oceans, and coastal regions.

# Bibliography of Books

Tundi Agardy

*Ocean Zoning: Making Marine Management More Effective.* London: Routledge, 2010.

Michelle Allsop, Stefan E. Pambuccian, Paul Johnston, and David Santillo

*State of the World's Oceans.* New York: Springer, 2010.

Donald C. Baur, Tim Eichenberg, and G. Michael Sutton

*Ocean and Coastal Law and Policy.* Chicago: American Bar Association, 2009.

Gregory Beaugrand

*Marine Biodiversity, Climatic Variability and Global Change.* London: Routledge, 2012.

Andrea Belgrano and Charles W. Fowler, eds.

*Ecosystem-Based Management for Marine Fisheries.* Cambridge: Cambridge University Press, 2011.

Mansel Blackford

*Making Seafood Sustainable: American Experiences in Global Perspective.* Philadelphia: University of Pennsylvania Press, 2012.

Stuart Bunting

*Principles of Sustainable Aquaculture: Promoting Social, Economic and Environmental Resilience.* London: Routledge, 2013.

Sara Cohen Christopherson

*Top 50 Reasons to Care About Whales and Dolphins: Animals in Peril.* Berkeley Heights, NJ: Enslow, 2010.

Joachim Claudet, ed. *Marine Protected Areas: A Multidisciplinary Approach*. Ecology, Biodiversity and Conservation series. Cambridge: Cambridge University Press, 2011.

Larry B. Crowder and Elliott A. Norse, eds. *Marine Conservation Biology: The Science of Maintaining the Sea's Biodiversity*. Washington, DC: Island, 2005.

Ted Danson and Michael D'Orso *Oceana: Our Endangered Oceans and What We Can Do to Save Them*. Emmaus, PA: Rodale, 2011.

Pedro Duarte and J. Magdalena Santana-Casiano *Oceans and the Atmospheric Carbon Content*. New York: Springer, 2010.

Sylvia Earle and Bill McKibben *The World Is Blue: How Our Fate and the Ocean's Are One*. Washington, DC: National Geographic, 2010.

Ronald Eisler *Ocean Acidification: A Comprehensive Overview*. Houston: Science, 2011.

Carmel Finley *All the Fish in the Sea: Maximum Sustainable Yield and the Failure of Fisheries Management*. Chicago: University of Chicago Press, 2011.

Katherine A. Green Hammond *Fisheries Management Under the Fishery Conservation and Management Act, the Marine Mammal Protection Act, and the Endangered Species Act*. Springfield, VA: Marine Mammal Commission, 1980.

Ray Hilborn — *Overfishing: What Everyone Needs to Know.* Oxford: Oxford University Press, 2012.

Cathryn Berger Kaye and Philippe Cousteau — *Going Blue: A Teen Guide to Saving Our Oceans, Lakes, Rivers & Wetlands.* Minneapolis: Free Spirit, 2010.

Richard Kensington, Laura Stocker, and David Wood, eds. — *Sustainable Coastal Management and Climate Adaptation: Global Lessons from Regional Approaches in Australia.* Boca Raton, FL: CRC Press, 2012.

Elena McCarthy — *International Regulation of Underwater Sound: Establishing Rules and Standards to Address Ocean Noise Pollution.* New York: Springer, 2010.

Karen McLeod and Heather Leslie, eds. — *Ecosystem-Based Management for the Oceans.* Washington, DC: Island, 2009.

Alanna Mitchell — *Seasick: Ocean Change and the Extinction of Life on Earth.* Chicago: University of Chicago Press, 2009.

Skye Moody — *Washed Up: The Curious Journeys of Flotsam and Jetsam.* Seattle: Sasquatch Books, 2006.

Charles Moore and Cassandra Phillips — *Plastic Ocean: How a Sea Captain's Chance Discovery Launched a Determined Quest to Save the Oceans.* New York: Penguin, 2011.

Jun Morikawa — *Whaling in Japan.* New York: Columbia University Press, 2009.

National Commission on the Deepwater Horizon Oil Spill and Offshore Drilling — *Deep Water: The Gulf Oil Disaster and the Future of BP Offshore Drilling*. Washington, DC: US Government Printing Office, 2011.

Kenneth Partridge, ed. — *The Politics of the Oceans*. New York: HW Wilson, 2011.

Daniel Pauly — *Five Easy Pieces: The Impact of Fisheries on Marine Ecosystems*. Washington, DC: Island, 2010.

Roger L. Reep and Robert K. Bonde — *The Florida Manatee: Biology and Conservation*. Gainesville: University Press of Florida, 2010.

Callum Roberts — *The Ocean of Life: The Fate of Man and the Sea*. New York: Viking, 2012.

David de Rothschild — *Plastiki: Across the Pacific on Plastic; An Adventure to Save Our Oceans*. San Francisco: Chronicle Books, 2011.

Carl Safina — *A Sea in Flames*. New York: Crown, 2011.

John Slade — *Climate Change and the Oceans*. Woodgate, NY: Woodgate International, 2010.

William W. Taylor, Abigail J. Lynch, and Michael G. Schechter, eds. — *Sustainable Fisheries: Multi-Level Approaches to a Global Problem*. Bethesda, MD: American Fisheries Society, 2011.

| US Senate Subcommittee on Oceans, Atmosphere, Fisheries, and Coast Guard | *The Future of Ocean Governance: Building Our National Ocean Policy: Hearing Before the Senate Subcommittee on Oceans, Atmosphere, Fisheries, and Coast Guard of the Committee on Commerce, Science, and Transportation*, 111th Congress. Washington, DC: US Government Printing Office, 2011. |

# Index